PUBLISHED
BY
H.F. WALLING
86 TROWBRIDGE ST
CAMBRIDGE, MASS.

1. Water-lilies, Cape Cod

"...Again I scent the white water-lily, and a season I had waited for is arrived.... What confirmation of our hope is in the fragrance of the water-lily! I shall not so soon despair of the world for it."

Thoreau's Cape Cod

With the early photographs of

Herbert W. Gleason

EDITED, WITH AN INTRODUCTION BY

Thea Wheelwright

BARRE PUBLISHERS

Barre, Massachusetts

1971

The photographs by Herbert W. Gleason have been printed from the collection of negatives owned by Roland W. Robbins.

International Standard Book Number 0–8271–7119–6
Library of Congress Card Number 79–163877
Copyright © 1971 by Barre Publishing Co., Incorporated

Design: Raymond M. Grimaila
Composition: Eastern Typesetting Company, Inc.
Printing: Eastern Press, Inc.
Binding: Stanhope Bindery, Inc.
Composed and printed in the United States.

Contents

Illustrations

Introduction

PROBABLY because for the most part they are not engaged with objects or people on Cape Cod but with the straightforward effort to show the reader exactly what Henry David Thoreau saw, Herbert Gleason's photographs not only re-created Thoreau's Cape Cod fifty-four years after his first visit there, but provide an aspect still true today if one leaves the highways and strikes out onto the back shore, or walks along the edge of the Bay. What changes man has brought about in the way of new structures cannot change the glorious framework of sea and sky that both men knew.

Thoreau does not specifically associate water lilies with Cape Cod, but I have chosen a portrait of them—one cannot call it anything less—as the first illustration in this book, for several reasons. It is an outstanding example of Gleason's photography; Thoreau devotes many passages in his Journals to his yearly delight in these flowers; and I associate them vividly with my own experience of the Cape.

Each year during the time I lived in Provincetown I waited for the familiar early-summer cry: "Wada-lilies! Wada-lilies! Ten-cents-a-bunch!" It came from a bright-faced, weatherbeaten gnome of a man, who trundled a wheelbarrow full of dewy blossoms up and down the streets. He was always dressed in very white sneakers and socks and washed-blue denim pants and jacket, and wore a peaked cap—all so extraordinarily clean and properly creased that, ancient and toothless as he was, he looked as though his mother had dressed him up to go out and do her errands. I can still hear his voice, and the chopped rhythm of his cry. I used to plummet down the stairs from where I lived on the top floor of one of the old houses on the water side of Commercial Street, and buy as many bunches as I could afford, and glory in their purity and their scent.

When I first went to Provincetown in 1929, it was still comparatively uncrowded. We spent a summer in a shack on the backshore a few years later, and my memories are crowned with such occasions as walking along the water's edge when dogfish were chasing silver perch on shore, and picking up our dinner, still flapping, broiling it outdoors, and tasting heaven in it with bread and wine, while the sun cast its saffron light on a subsiding sea. I remember digging up clams and quahogs from their easily spotted shelters along the hard beach, especially in an easterly wind; or buying a bucket of oysters or scallops in the shell at Wellfleet, before eel grass disappeared from the Bay. I remember one perfect September day late in the month, when I went blueberrying with a friend in the woods back of town. The air was so cold and crisp I wished for a head scarf, yet the berries were sprinkling their bright blue against the russet and green land. They were deliciously cold to the touch, though each time I bent down to pick one, the earth gave out a bayberry scented warmth. I wanted to lie down in that warmth and I finally did. It was wonderful! The moss and lichen, minute, bright scarlet specks and gray cups on soft green, and almost microscopic bone-white formations springing up here and there, gave my eyes a feast I could not have enjoyed from a normal height.

But Thoreau did not stay on the Cape long enough to savor the peculiar quality of these joys, tempered always by sight and sound of the sea. He went merely "wishing to get a better view . . . of the ocean" and this he did. He spent most of the time walking in the course of four visits, about one month in all—October 1849, June 1850, July 1855, and June 1857—twice with his friend, the poet William Ellery Channing, and twice alone. He saw the countryside, the trees and plants that bloomed in June, July, and October; he spoke with people who lived nearer the ocean than the Bay, and avoided the villages, except for Provincetown itself, where he took a boat back to Boston.

He walked from Eastham to Provincetown "twice on the Atlantic side, and once on the Bay side also, excepting four or five miles, and crossed the Cape half a dozen times" on the way. "But having come so fresh to the sea," he writes, "I have got but little salted. My readers must expect only so much saltness as the land breeze acquires from blowing over an arm of the sea, or is tasted on the windows and the bark of trees twenty miles inland, after September gales."[1]

Cape Cod, I believe, was an interlude for Thoreau, a relaxation from an arduous task he had set upon himself. It was the subject for a book at a time when he still thought in terms of earning part of his living through writing (when he had to buy back 706 copies of *A Week on the Concord and Merrimack Rivers*, of which only 1000 had been printed, he more or less gave up this dream). Actually the text for his book on the Cape was created primarily from field notes made on his first three trips. The first four chapters were "printed by their author in *Putnam's Magazine* in 1855," according to an Introductory Note in the Riverside Press limited edition of *Thoreau's Writings*, published in 1894. But the completed book appeared posthumously. He used some of the material also for Lyceum lectures, and his audiences were convulsed by his stories of the "Wellfleet Oysterman."

Thoreau's trips to the Cape were voyages of discovery in one sense, and of research into a part of America's past, but one does not have the feeling that the impact of what he saw went very deep. Concord was Thoreau's home, and the river and ponds around it were his passion. His most eloquent expressions of life come in his Journal entries about walks in these areas rather than along the beaches and through the woods of Cape Cod.

Thus the book differs from his other works, which were the vehicles of carefully pruned thoughts upon the subjects that run through his Journals like roads that he crossed over and over in his exploration of the meaning of life and death. *Cape Cod* is a tale told more on the surface than the rest of his writings; it is composed of practical observations and on-the-spot human encounters and anecdotes. Yet even this volume is not a consecutive narrative of discovery, but is pieced together, partly from his Journal, his practice-book, and partly from field notes. Two sentences of one paragraph in the Journal go into the make-up of pages as disparate as 185 and 271 of the book. They are fitted exactly into an intricate mosaic, the shape of all his writing. And this book bears the stamp, also, though in lesser degree than his *Week on the Concord and Merrimack Rivers,* of the kind of vision he writes of many times: "I find the actual to be far less real to me than the imagined.... This stream of events which we consent to call actual, and that other mightier stream which alone carries us with it,—what makes the difference? On the one our bodies float, and we have sympathy with it through them; on the other our spirits. We are ever dying to one world and being born into another, and possibly no man knows whether he is at any time dead in the sense in which he affirms that phenomenon of another, or not. Our thoughts are the epochs of our life: all else is but as a journal of the winds that blew while we were here."[2]

"My profession," he remarks in his journal in 1851, "is to be always on the alert to find God in nature, to know his lurking-places, to attend all the oratorios, the operas, in nature.[3]

"... Facts should be only as the frames to my pictures; they should be material to the mythology which I am writing; not facts to assist men to make money, farmers to farm profitably, in any common sense; facts to tell who I am, and where I have been or what I have thought.... My facts shall be falsehoods to the common sense.... Facts which the mind perceived, thoughts which the body thought,—with these I deal. I, too, cherish vague and misty forms, vaguest when the cloud at which I gaze is dissipated quite and naught but the skyey depths are seen."[4]

And in the spring of 1853, when masses of golden willow were "conspicuous against the distant, still half-russet hills and forests," he writes: "He is the richest who has most use for nature as raw material of tropes and symbols with which to describe his life. If these gates of golden willows affect me, they correspond to the beauty and promise of some experience on which I am entering. If I am overflowing with life, am rich in experience for which I lack expression, then nature will be my language full of poetry,—all nature will *fable,* and every natural phenomenon be a myth...."[5]

Herbert Wendell Gleason (1855–1937) followed in Thoreau's footsteps and tried literally to catch the exact scenes Thoreau either describes or had to pass because of the routes he took. In a book he wrote entitled *Through the Year with Thoreau,* Gleason writes in his Foreword: "With respect to the photographs, it may be said that they were taken by the author with the sole purpose of securing, in every case, as close a correspondence as possible with Thoreau's description. Artistic considerations were wholly secondary."[6] Probably the photographs he took during the fall of 1903 on Cape Cod were done in the same spirit. He wanted his camera to take the place of Thoreau's eyes and put the reader in a position to look at scenes and objects from the same angles of sky and sea that Thoreau himself saw them. And because he was a fine photographer, no matter how secondary the artistic consideration, Gleason's work reveals an inherent beauty.

The facts known about him are few. He was born in Malden, Massachusetts, on June 5, 1855, the son of Herbert Gleason of Plymouth and Elizabeth Upton of Wakefield, Massachusetts. He went to public schools in Malden, and graduated from Williams College in 1877. He decided upon the ministry, went to Union Seminary in 1878, was Resident Licentiate at Andover Seminary in 1882. He married his childhood sweetheart Lulie W. Rounds of Malden in 1883, and they lived in Pelican Rapids, Minnesota, for their first two years of married life. He was ordained in 1887, while Pastor of the Como Avenue Church in Minneapolis, and he served as editor of the *Northwestern Congregationalist* (later the *Kingdom*) from 1888 to 1899. In this year Gleason gave up the ministry and began to devote himself to photography, on which he must have spent his previous leisure hours, for it evidently had become his passion. From then on, the Gleasons lived in Boston and he traveled extensively with his camera, delivered lectures, and wrote articles which he illustrated with his work.

His travel schedule soon begins to read like a business executive's appointment calendar: "Interior of Parlor & Hall, 1815 Columbus Avenue, Minneapolis, 2/2/99; Interior of Mr. Gilbert's home in Duluth, 2/5/99; Logging Train on Trestle, Knife Run, Minnesota, 2/8/99." Each of his photographs was carefully labeled and dated. By the fall of 1899, he was in the east shooting pictures of Walden Pond.

Between 1900 and 1916, in addition to his New England forays, Gleason made two trips to Alaska, six to California and the Pacific Coast, three to the Grand Canyon; seven to the Canadian Rockies; two to Yellowstone Park; and three to Colorado on picture assignments, either of his own choosing or, one supposes, for payment. The man must have spent a good portion of his life in railway cars and coaches, and finally in slow-paced automobiles, to have traveled so much distance.

In April 1908, Mr. Gleason presented an illustrated lecture on "The Glories of the Sierras" to 1000 members and friends of the Appalachian Mountain Club, of which he was himself a member. In November of 1915, he presented a series of eight lectures on "The National Parks of America" at the Tremont Temple in Boston. Many of the slides for these lectures were handcolored by his wife.

He became somewhat of a horticulturist himself as a result of his interest in the careers of several naturalists besides Thoreau. He became a friend of Luther Burbank, and worked with John Burroughs and John Muir as well. His photographs were used to illustrate articles in the *National Geographic* and other magazines, and for the 20-volume 1906 edition Houghton Mifflin did of Thoreau's *Writings*. Gleason died at the age of 82 in 1937, having lost his wife four years before that. Up to the last month of his life he was still active in his chosen field.

So much for the record, but nothing about the man himself. One can only conjecture. Scant as they are, the facts point at least to a religious bent and a love of nature. Since Gleason had the courage to leave the ministry and change his way of life entirely at the age of 44, he must have had something of the independent spirit Thoreau had. Whether he actually turned against formal religion, as Thoreau obviously did, we do not know.

Even in *Cape Cod* Thoreau gibes at the church in such passages as the one in which he compares it with the windmill. In his Journals he was more specific. In December 1856, he notes, "Lectured in basement (vestry) of the orthodox church, and I trust helped to undermine it."[7] And two months later: ". . . in the clergyman of the most liberal sort I see no perfectly independent human nucleus, but I seem to see some indistinct scheme hovering about, to which he has lent himself, to which he belongs. It is a very fine cobweb in the lower stratum of the air, which stronger wings do not even discover. Whatever he may say, he does not know that one day is as good as another. Whatever he may say, he does not know that a man's creed can never be written, that there are no particular expressions of belief that deserve to be prominent... What great interval is there between him who is caught in Africa and made a plantation slave of in the South, and him who is caught in New England and made a Unitarian minister of? In course of time they will abolish the one form of servitude, and, not long after, the other...."[8]

One wonders: Did Herbert Gleason think of the ministry as a form of slavery?

Whatever his reasons for leaving it, he had become a great admirer of Thoreau, and his photographs create a framework for Thoreau's approach to nature.

These two men—one essentially unknown except for the creations that came from his camera, the other a sturdy, earthbound yet cosmi-conscious recorder of Nature, who seems at times entangled in the endless detail which he evidently hoped to turn into an integrated whole, a revelation of Nature's intent—come together in this book on an unequal footing. The photographs speak for Gleason. But *Cape Cod*—if one had access to no other writings of Thoreau—does not speak fully for the author. He paid small tithe to the almighty dollar; he escaped the marketplace most of the time—gave few hours to pencil making, teaching and surveying, and writing for publication; but this book, I believe, was part of it. Not that it was undertaken begrudgingly: except for the opening chapter with its grim details of the wreckage of the "St. John," *Cape Cod* is written with cheerful gusto.

Like so many of us who long for creative leisure but have gotten ourselves trapped in day-to-day trivia that bear the dollar sign,

Thoreau, though occupied the way he wanted to be, lost himself much of the time in minutiae.

His passion for detail had an almost obsessional quality. It is as though he were trying to describe and classify every single shell on a beach, no matter how minute.

I remember taking time on the beach to look, really *look* at a grain of sand, and being subject at the same time to sea and sky and wind and, above all, sound. While I examined that one small particle closely, I became part of it and part of the whole surrounding, and my thoughts encompassed not only that moment but the fabric of my whole life. It was this kind of integration that Thoreau's way of life gave him constantly. Most of us experience it only on rare occasions. It was because of his stubborn intensity in staying with his thing that, although he did not round out his enormous project, everything Thoreau wrote has the permanence of a grain of sand, and is always being scanned by others who seek a better way of life.

Sometimes while reading passages in his Journal, I had the feeling that his observations were like the undermovements of a woman's life, busy with small household detail while her mind works at something else. Thoreau's thoughts upon art, writing, world problems, God, death, would push themselves up through all botanical detail, with no introduction at all, and subside again beneath the next observation, as though there had been no interruption.

Yet at times it seemed as though he were deliberately trying to catch every sight and thought on the wing, deliberately, not accidentally, recording them in a "stream-of-consciousness" sequence. It is this sudden interpolation, with seldom an apparent connection between it and surrounding botanical detail, that makes one realize Thoreau must have planned to reorganize the entire Journal at some time into that mythology he dreamt of. He would make on-the-spot notes, often scribbling by moonlight, about what he saw. Whether he jotted down key words or phrases from a subterranean layer of thoughts at the same time and elaborated upon these later when copying botanical observa-

2. Looking east across Pleasant Bay at South Orleans (11/19/03)

Pleasant Bay cuts a wide piece out of the eastern coastline of the Cape, between North Chatham and South Orleans, and forces Route 28 to close in toward Route 6, which it joins at Orleans. From there on, combined routes continue through the center of the Cape to its tip—a broad modern highway. But an alternate, old route still twines its way from town to town on the Bay side, and the backshore is still dominated by the high cliffs and barren lands and sea. T.W.

tions into his Journal, or interrupted his copying—which could have been a rather mechanical process—to record his thoughts as they came, one does not know. He cautioned himself to practice "a true sauntering of the eye"[9] and perhaps this is the key: a sauntering of the mind as well. But it was not an unconscious meandering: "While dropping beans in the garden ... I hear from across the fields the note of the bay-wing [Thoreau's name for a vesper sparrow], ... and it instantly translates me from the sphere of my work and repairs all the world that we jointly inhabit. ... The spirit of its earth-song, of its serene and true philosophy, was breathed into me, and I saw the world as through a glass, as it lies eternally. ...

"I ordinarily plod along a sort of whitewashed prison entry, subject to some indifferent or even grovelling mood. I do not distinctly realize my destiny. I have turned down my light to the merest glimmer and am doing some task which I have set myself. I take incredibly narrow views, live on the limits, and have no recollection of absolute truth. Mushroom institutions hedge me in. But suddenly, in some fortunate moment, the voice of eternal wisdom reaches me, even in the strain of the sparrow, and liberates me, whets and clarifies my senses, makes me a competent witness."[10]

Often he wrote the same idea down, not once but two or three times in the same passage—put there for him to come back to and polish finally into the kind of sentences he demanded of himself: "... Sentences which suggest far more than they say, which have an atmosphere about them, which do not merely report an old, but make a new, impression; sentences which suggest as many things and are as durable as a Roman aqueduct; to frame these," he wrote, "that is the *art* of writing.[11] ...

"Whatever things I perceive with my entire man, those let me record, and it will be poetry. The sounds which I hear with the consent and coincidence of all my senses, these are significant and musical; at least, they only are heard."[12]

Thoreau, (1817–1862), who lived less than fifty years, must have realized for some time before he died that he would never finish his task. He could only keep on with it doggedly.

". . . A broad margin of leisure is as beautiful in a man's life as in a book. . ." he wrote.

". . . That aim in life is highest which requires the highest and finest discipline. How much, what infinite, leisure it requires, as of a lifetime, to appreciate a single phenomenon! You must . . . give yourself wholly to it. . . ."[13]

". . . However, you will not see these splendors, whether you stand on the hilltop or in the hollow, unless you are prepared to see them. . . . The beauty of the earth answers exactly to your demand and appreciation."[14]

We see in Nature whatever we seek. It is all there. We dream and anticipate, then find. And the dream, in a sense, creates what we will find.

"It is only when we forget all our learning that we begin to know. . . . To conceive of it [any natural object] with a total apprehension I must for the thousandth time approach it as something totally strange. . . ."[15]

Thoreau embraced so completely the individual's needs for independence that he has become a standard ever since upon which reformers could lean. Each generation knows this man as one to whose writings they can turn and find relevant material. What could be more apt than this for today's ecology-oriented? "What sort of cultivation, or civilization and improvement, is ours to boast of, if it turns out that, as in this instance, unhandselled nature is worth more even by our modes of valuation than our improvements are,—if we leave the land poorer than we found it? Is it good economy, to try it by the lowest standards, to cut down all our forests, if a forest will pay into the town treasury a greater tax than the farms which may supplant it,—if the oaks by steadily growing according to their nature leave our improvements in the rear?"[16]

Civil rights, the need for a sense of dignity and purpose in labor, and the need for creative leisure are other examples.

"Talk about slavery! It is not the peculiar institution of the South," he wrote in December 1860. "It exists wherever men are bought and sold, wherever a man allows himself to be made a mere thing or a tool, and surrenders his inalienable rights of reason and conscience. Indeed, this slavery is more complete than that which enslaves the body alone. . . ."[17]

". . . Every man, and the woodchopper among the rest, should love his work as much as the poet does his. All good political arrangements proceed on this supposition. If labor mainly, or to any considerable degree, serves the purpose of a police, to keep men out of mischief, it indicates a rottenness at the foundation of our community."[18]

Henry Thoreau was so far ahead of his time in facing these problems in *practice* that it will probably be another ten or twenty years before our society even begins to catch up with him. He suffered privation and, deepest-cutting of all, ridicule, to live the life he believed in. He worked only so much as needed in exchange for leisure. What man consciously does that today? Except for some of the younger people who have broken away from tradition, and artists of all ages, most men still work with the idea of earning a period of leisure at the *end* of their lives. He took his all along, but used every instant of it to put down everything that he saw—not just surface-seeing, but through layer upon layer. As one reads his Journals it is as though one were following a person who was playing upon five instruments at once, each representing one of the senses, and all in concert—sight and sound the major and minor melodies above the rest.

Yet in 1852 he had become a battlefield in himself between poetry and science, and he already believed himself—the poet—the loser. "I have a commonplace-book for facts and another for poetry," he writes, "but I find it difficult always to preserve the vague distinction which I had in mind, for the most interesting and beautiful facts are so much the more poetry and that is their success. They are *translated* from earth to heaven. I see that if my facts were sufficiently vital and significant,—perhaps transmuted more into the substance of the human mind, —I should need but one book of poetry to contain them all."[19] Then he writes later, under the same date: "It is impossible for the same person to see things from the poet's point of view and that of the man of science. The poet's second love may be science, not his first,—when use has worn off the bloom . . ."[20]

"The strains from my muse are as rare nowadays, or of late years," he wrote on the following day, "as the notes of birds in the winter,— the faintest occasional tinkling sound, and mostly of the woodpecker kind or the harsh jay or crow. It never melts into a song. Only the *day-day-day* of an inquisitive titmouse."[21] A bitter self-evaluation!

I believe Henry Thoreau was aware that he had trapped himself in his Journal, but kept piling detail upon detail in a kind of monumental stubbornness—at first with the hope of producing a *new being,* a new myth in which the language of Nature would be combined with that of human thought in a new, organic whole. Later, it was with a kind of despair.

But for the reader Thoreau's often botany-burdened Journal is filled with superb narrative gems about birds and animals and trees and flowers. Such are his descriptions of the "splendid male humming-bird coming zigzag in long tacks, like a bee, but far swifter, along the edge of the swamp, in hot haste";[22] of the snapping turtle, "who was before Columbus, perchance. Grown, not gray, but green with the lapse of ages";[23] of the felling of a noble pine: "And now it fans the hillside with its fall, and it lies down to its bed in the valley, from which it is never to rise, as softly as a feather, folding its green mantle about it like a warrior, as if, tired of standing, it embraced the earth with silent joy, returning its elements to the dust again. But hark! there you only saw, but did not hear. There now comes up a deafening crash . . . even trees do not die without a groan";[24] of "a softer, flowing, curling warble, like a purling stream"[25] of the bluebird on the spring air; of a soaring hawk: ". . . The poetry of motion. Not as preferring one place to another, but enjoying each as long as possible";[26] or of the cricket song: "no transient love-strain, hushed when the incubating season is past, but a glorifying of God and enjoying of him forever."[27]

The Journal is filled also with sudden fierce ruminations, in the anguish his concept of friendship so often brought him. This, for example, upon "decaying friendship" (surely he must have meant love) : "...Morning, noon, and night, I suffer a physical pain, an aching of the breast which unfits me for my tasks ... I feel like a wreck that is driving before the gale ... my seams open, my timbers laid bare ..."[28]—sandwiched, incidentally, in a description of two yellow-spotted tortoises; or in his fiery ache and wrath over the hanging of John Brown: "When I hear of John Brown and his wife weeping at length, it is as if the rocks sweated";[29] or in his conclusion: "It matters not where or how far you travel,—the farther commonly the worse,—but how much alive you are.... All that a man has to say or do that can possibly concern mankind, is in some shape or other to tell the story of his love,—to sing; and, if he is fortunate and keeps alive, he will be forever in love. This alone is to be alive to the extremities."[30]

The variety is endless, and it is tempting to go on offering sample after sample. But to get back to the subject of this introductory essay:

If Thoreau's trip to the Cape which began October 9, 1849, with his friend Channing, was actually his first sight of the ocean, he saw it at its most magnificent and ruthless. The two men went by way of Cohasset, for a violent storm not only had kept the Provincetown steamer from running, but had cause the wreck three days before of the brig "St. John," from Galway, Ireland, with the death of 145 immigrants. Rather than wait in Boston for the storm to subside, Thoreau and his companion decided to join the relatives and friends who took "the cars" to view the wreck, or identify the bodies, or attend the mass funeral which was to be held that afternoon.

Thoreau's description of the scenes they witnessed is good, crisp journalism. Like all of his writings, *Cape Cod* showed complete mastery of the polished, succinct sentence:

... It was now Tuesday morning, and the sea was still breaking violently on the rocks. There were eighteen or twenty of the same large boxes that I have mentioned, lying on a green hillside, a few rods from the water, and surrounded by a crowd. The bodies which had been recovered, twenty-seven or eight in all, had been collected there. Some were rapidly nailing down the lids, others were carting the boxes away, and others were lifting the lids, which were yet loose, and peeping under the cloths, for each body, with such rags as still adhered to it, was covered loosely with a white sheet. I witnessed no signs of grief, but there was a sober dispatch of business which was affecting. One man was seeking to identify a particular body, and one undertaker or carpenter was calling to another to know in what box a certain child was put. I saw many marble feet and matted heads as the cloths were raised, and one livid, swollen, and mangled body of a drowned girl,—who probably had intended to go out to service in some American family,—to which some rags still adhered, with a string, half concealed by the flesh, about its swollen neck; the coiled-up wreck of a human hulk, gashed by the rocks or fishes, so that the bone and muscle were exposed, but quite bloodless,—merely red and white,—with wide-open and staring eyes, yet lustreless, dead-lights; or like the cabin windows of a stranded vessel, filled with sand. Sometimes there were two or more children, or a parent and child, in the same box, and on the lid would perhaps be written with red chalk, 'Bridget such-a-one, and sister's child.' . . .[31]

. . . In the very midst of the crowd about this wreck, there were men with carts busily collecting the seaweed which the storm had cast up, and conveying it beyond the reach of the tide, though they were often obliged to separate fragments of clothing from it, and they might at any moment have found a human body under it. Drown who might, they did not forget that this weed was a valuable manure. This shipwreck had not produced a visible vibration in the fabric of society.

About a mile south we could see, rising above the rocks, the masts of the British brig which the St. John had endeavored to follow, which had slipped her cables, and, by good luck, run into the mouth of Cohasset Harbor. A little further along the shore we saw a man's clothes on a rock; further, a woman's scarf, a gown, a straw bonnet, the brig's caboose, and one of her masts high and dry, broken into several pieces. In another rocky cove, several rods from the water, and behind rocks twenty feet high, lay a part of one side of the vessel, still hanging together. It was, perhaps, forty feet long, by fourteen wide. I was even more surprised at the power of the waves, exhibited on this shattered fragment, than I had been at the sight of the smaller fragments before. The largest timbers and iron braces were broken superfluously, and I saw that no material could withstand the power of the waves; that iron must go to pieces in such a case, and an iron vessel would be cracked up like an egg-shell on the rocks. Some of these timbers, however, were so rotten that I could almost thrust my umbrella through them. They told us that some were saved on this piece, and also showed where the sea had heaved it into this cove which was now dry. When I saw where it had come in, and in what condition, I wondered that any had been saved on it. A little further on a crowd of men was collected around the mate of the St. John, who was telling his story. He was a slim-looking youth, who spoke of the captain as the master, and seemed a little excited. He was saying that when they jumped into the boat, she filled, and, the vessel lurching, the weight of the water in the boat caused the painter to break, and so they were separated. Whereat one man came away, saying,—

"Well, I don't see but he tells a straight story enough. You see, the weight of the water in the boat broke the painter. A boat full of water is very heavy,'—and so on, in a loud and impertinently earnest tone, as if he had a bet depending on it, but had no humane interest in the matter.

"Another, a large man, stood near by upon a rock, gazing into the sea, and chewing large quids of tobacco, as if that habit were forever confirmed with him.

'Come,' says another to his companion, 'let's be off. We've seen the whole of it. It's no use to stay to the funeral.'"[32]

Thoreau was surprised at his own reactions to the sea's immense power and carelessness of human life, and to the disregard for both on the part of some of the spectators.

On the whole, it was not so impressive a scene as I might have expected. If I had found one body cast upon the beach in some lonely place, it would have affected me more. I sympathized rather with the winds and waves, as if to toss and mangle these poor human bodies was the order of the day.

If this was the law of Nature, why waste any time in awe or pity? If the last day were come, we should not think so much about the separation of friends or the blighted prospects of individuals. I saw that corpses might be multiplied, as on the field of battle, till they no longer affected us in any degree, as exceptions to the common lot of humanity. Take all the graveyards together, they are always the majority. It is the individual and private that demands our sympathy. A man can attend but one funeral in the course of his life, can behold but one corpse. Yet I saw that the inhabitants of the shore would be not a little affected by this event. They would watch there many days and nights for the sea to give up its dead, and their imaginations and sympathies would supply the place of mourners far away, who as yet knew not of the wreck. . . . I saw that the beauty of the shore itself was wrecked for many a lonely walker there, until he could perceive, at last, how its beauty was enhanced by wrecks like this, and it acquired thus a rarer and sublimer beauty still.

Why care for these dead bodies? They really have no friends but the worms or fishes. Their owners were coming to the New World, as Columbus and the Pilgrims did,—they were within a mile of its shores; but, before they could reach it, they emigrated to a newer world than ever Columbus dreamed of, yet one of whose existence we believe that there is far more universal and convincing evidence—though it has not yet been discovered by science—than Columbus had of this: not merely mariners' tales and some paltry drift-wood and seaweed, but a continual drift and instinct to all our shores. . . ."[33]

The two men left the scene of the wreck and spent the night in Bridgewater, then took the cars to Sandwich, "the terminus of the 'Cape Cod Railroad,' though but the beginning of the Cape," as Thoreau remarks. At that point their journey down the Cape really began; and a new, lighthearted tone pervades what becomes in part the journal of their trip and in part a history of, and descriptive guide to, the major towns and ports of the Cape, which Thoreau early defined in a metaphor that has become a classic in itself:

Cape Cod is the bared and bended arm of Massachusetts: the shoulder is at Buzzard's Bay; the elbow, or crazy-bone, at Cape Mallebarre; the wrist at Truro; and the sandy fist at Provincetown,—behind which the State stands on her guard, with her back to the Green Mountains, and her feet planted on the floor of the ocean, like an athlete protecting her Bay,—boxing with northeast storms, and, ever and anon, heaving up her Atlantic adversary from the lap of earth,—ready to thrust forward her other fist, which keeps guard the while upon her breast at Cape Ann.[34]

They took the stagecoach, which followed what is now Route 6A, to Orleans, and from there took to the back shore on foot. Thus they by-passed the towns along what is now Route 28 on Nantucket Sound.

Herbert Gleason, starting out also in October (the 20th), some fifty-four years later, evidently started from Orleans and spent that day and the next going down-Cape along the coast of Eastham, the Nauset Plains and Wellfleet; then on to Provincetown where he spent a day along the back shore (which there faces northwest) and in the town proper; then back up the outer beaches to Highland Light and the Truro area on the 23rd. He came back a week later (October 30) to get a few more pictures of the Eastham area, and made a further trip on November 19 and 20, when he worked from South Orleans back up the Cape to the Harwiches. It is from this latter group of pictures, the most dramatic of the Cape Cod collection to which we had access, that we have selected illustrations for that part of the trip during which Thoreau and Channing supposedly saw mere glimpses of the Bay-shore road and villages through rain-obscured windows, while they read about the area so magnificently portrayed by Gleason.

Oddly enough, there are no pictures of the towns on the old coach route, except for Provincetown itself; nor are there photographs of gulls and beach birds, whose sounds are as much a part of the Cape as the sea itself. One cannot visualize a Cape sky without gulls dipping and tossing and sliding on the wind, their beaks describing tireless arcs while they search for fish below; or remember early morning sounds without including their shrill metallic clamor, scrapping over "gurrah" thrown overboard by fishermen returning from their weirs. Nor do Gleason's photographs show wild seascapes like those Thoreau describes on this whole first journey, which began with a storm and ended in a stinging northeast wind: "... The air was filled with dust like snow, and cutting sand which made the face tingle, and we saw what it must be to face it when the weather was drier, and, if possible, windier still,—to face a migrating sand-bar in the air, which has picked up its duds and is off,—to be whipped with a cat, not o' nine-tails, but of a myriad of tails, and each one a sting to it. ..."[35]

Perhaps Gleason's camera would have been blown down, or the lens pitted by the sand, had he attempted such pictures. The lack of modern camera equipment may have determined against his taking birds in flight also.

Yet, though it would be fairly easy to take pictures of the back shore without birds in them, it would actually be *difficult* to catch a scene on the Bay side without gulls being part of it. Gleason would surely have seen some on their accustomed perches atop wharf posts or weir poles!

We can only guess at the explanation for this lack, since so little is known of Mr. Gleason. A series of plates devoted specifically to sea-birds might have been lost; or some individual—probably unaware of the valuable cache in his attic—may own another collection of Gleason plates that would fill in the gap; or Gleason may have disliked scavenger birds and avoided taking pictures of them. But the latter would hardly seem to be valid, for surely, having shown himself to be such an admirer of Thoreau and having in his own book declared his intention to show through the eye of his camera as much as he could of what Thoreau saw, it would be strange indeed if he had allowed personal prejudice to interfere with his purpose. Nevertheless it is extraordinary that not one bird is to be seen in these plates.*

Where clouds were concerned, Herbert Gleason fully sympathized with Thoreau's fascination, as the first series of illustrations in this

---

*Mr. Roland W. Robbins, owner of the collection from which these pictures were selected, reports that he could find only a few plates, out of some 6,000, which show gulls, and that were not taken on the Cape.

volume proves. And here, perhaps, is a backhand confirmation of our conjecture concerning the governing limits of his photographic equipment, for clouds move, but theirs is a constant, majestic slow-motion.

But let us get on with Thoreau's own, now cheerful account of the voyage he took with his friend "to get a better view" of the mighty ocean.

Thoreau's Cape Cod

with the early photographs of

Herbert W. Gleason

... As it rained hard, with driving mists, and there was no sign of its holding up, we here* took that almost obsolete conveyance, the stage, for "as far as it went that day," as we told the driver. We had forgotten how far a stage could go in a day, but we were told that the Cape roads were very "heavy," though they added that being of sand, the rain would improve them. This coach was an exceedingly narrow one, but as there was a slight spherical excess over two on a seat, the driver waited till nine passengers had got in, without taking the measure of any of them, and then shut the door after two or three ineffectual slams, as if the fault were all in the hinges or the latch,—while we timed our inspirations and expirations so as to assist him. . . .

Our route was along the Bay side, through Barnstable, Yarmouth, Dennis, and Brewster, to Orleans, with a range of low hills on our right, running down the Cape.**

---

*At Sandwich.

**Thoreau used the device of quoting from various old volumes to provide historical background or describe towns that lay parallel on the ocean side to the towns they went through along the Bay. T.W.

3. Sunset from outlet of Mill Pond, Chatham (11/19/03)
"It was in harmony with this fair evening that we ... moved ... without a jar over the liquid and almost invisible surface, floating directly toward those islands of the blessed which we call clouds in the sunset sky."

The weather was not favorable for wayside views, but we made the most of such glimpses of land and water as we could get through the rain. The country was, for the most part, bare, or with only a little scrubby wood left on the hills. . . . The sand by the roadside was partially covered with bunches of a moss-like plant, *Hudsonia tomentosa,* which a woman in the stage told us was called "poverty grass," because it grew where nothing else would.

I was struck by the pleasant equality which reigned among the stage company, and their broad and invulnerable good humor. They were what is called free and easy, and met one another to advantage, as men who had, at length, learned how to live. They appeared to know each other when they were strangers, they were so simple and downright. They were well met, in an unusual sense, that is, they met as well as they could meet, and did not seem to be troubled with any impediment. They were not afraid nor ashamed of one another, but were contented to make just such a company as the ingredients allowed.

4. Harwich Port from the Cove (11/20/03)

"... The grass had the same fresh green, and the distant herbage and foliage in the horizon the same dark blue, and the clouds and sky the same bright colors beautifully mingled and dissolving into one another, that I have seen in pictures of tropical landscapes and skies."

It was evident that the same foolish respect was not here claimed, for mere wealth and station, that is in many parts of New England; yet some of them were the "first people," as they are called, of the various towns through which we passed. Retired sea-captains, in easy circumstances, who talked of farming as sea-captains are wont; an erect, respectable, and trustworthy-looking man, in his wrapper, some of the salt of the earth, who had formerly been the salt of the sea; or a more courtly gentleman, who, perchance, had been a representative to the General Court in his day; or a broad, red-faced, Cape Cod man, who had seen too many storms to be easily irritated; or a fisherman's wife, who had been waiting a week for a coaster to leave Boston, and had at length come by the cars. . . .

Still we kept on in the rain, or, if we stopped, it was commonly at a post-office, and we thought that writing letters, and sorting them against our arrival, must be the principal employment of the inhabitants of the Cape this rainy day. The post-office appeared a singularly domestic institution here. Ever and anon the stage stopped before some low shop or dwelling, and a wheelwright or shoemaker appeared in his shirt-sleeves and leather apron, with spectacles newly donned, holding up Uncle Sam's bag, as if it were a slice of home-made cake, for the travelers, while he retailed some piece of gossip to the driver, really as indifferent to the presence of the former as if they were so much baggage. In one instance, we understood that a woman was the post-mistress, and they said that she made the best one on the road; but we suspected that the letters must be subjected to a very close scrutiny there. . . .

5. Sandy road through woods, Harwich Port to Harwich Centre
(11/20/03)

   "At length, seeing no end to the woods, laying down my pack, I
climbed an oak and looked off; but the woods bounded the horizon as
far as I could see on every side."

6. Fish trap and boat in Harwich Port (11/20/03)

7. Cloud effects looking west from Exchange Building in Harwich (11/20/03)

"...If there is nothing new on earth, still the traveler always has a resource in the skies. They are constantly turning a new page to view. The winds sets the type on this blue ground, and the inquiring may always read a new truth there...."

. . . At Dennis, we ventured to put our heads out of the windows, to see where we were going, and saw rising before us, through the mist, singular barren hills, all stricken with poverty-grass, looming up as if they were in the horizon, though they were close to us, and we seemed to have got to the end of the land on that side, notwithstanding that the horses were still headed that way. Indeed, that part of Dennis which we saw was an exceedingly barren and desolate country, of a character which I can find no name for; such a surface, perhaps, as the bottom of the sea made dry land day before yesterday. It was covered with poverty-grass, and there was hardly a tree in sight, but here and there a little weather-stained, one-storied house, with a red roof,—for often the roof was painted, though the rest of the house was not,—standing bleak and cheerless, yet with a broad foundation to the land, where the comfort must have been all inside. . . .

8. Looking south, over the Sound, from South Chatham (11/20/03)
"It is a place far away, yet actual and where we have been . . . Certain coincidences like this are accompanied by a certain flash as of hazy lightning, flooding all the world suddenly with a tremulous serene light which it is difficult to see long at a time."

... We read that "fogs are more frequent in Chatham than in any other part of the country; and they serve in summer, instead of trees, to shelter the houses against the heat of the sun. To those who delight in extensive vision,"—is it to be inferred that the inhabitants of Chatham do not?—"they are unpleasant, but they are not found to be unhealthful." Probably, also, the unobstructed sea-breeze answers the purpose of a fan. The historian of Chatham says further, that "in many families there is no difference between the breakfast and supper; cheese, cakes, and pies being as common at the one as at the other." But that leaves us still uncertain whether they were really common at either.

The road, which was quite hilly, here ran near the Bay-shore having the Bay on one side, and "the rough hill of Scargo," said to be the highest land on the Cape, on the other. Of the wide prospect of the Bay afforded by the summit of this hill, our guide says, "The view has not much of the beautiful in it, but it communicates a strong emotion of the sublime." That is the kind of communication which we love to have made to us. . . .

9. Down Muddy Creek toward Pleasant Bay, Chatham Port (11/19/03)

"... I heard the voices of men shouting aboard a vessel, half a mile from the shore, which sounded as if they were in a barn in the country, they being between the sails. It was a purely rural sound. As I looked over the water, I saw ... the sea nibbling voraciously at the continent. ..."

10. First view of Pleasant Bay, South Orleans (11/19/03) [Gleason is
seeing it from the north on his way to the Harwiches. T.W.]

"A field of water betrays the spirit that is in the air. It has new life
and motion. It is intermediate between land and sky. On land, only the
grass and trees wave, but the water itself is *rippled* by the wind. I see
the breeze dash across it in streaks and flakes of light. . . ."

At length, we stopped for the night at Higgins's tavern, in Orleans, feeling very much as if we were on a sand-bar in the ocean, and not knowing whether we should see land or water ahead when the mist cleared away. . . .

The next morning, Thursday, October 11, it rained as hard as ever; but we were determined to proceed on foot, nevertheless. . . . For the first four or five miles we followed the road, which here turns to the north on the elbow,—the narrowest part of the Cape,—that we might clear an inlet from the ocean, a part of Nauset Harbor, in Orleans, on our right. We found the traveling good enough for walkers on the sides of the roads, though it was "heavy" for horses in the middle. We walked with our umbrellas behind us since it blowed hard as well as rained, with driving mists, as the day before, and the wind helped us over the sand at a rapid rate. Everything indicated that we had reached a strange shore. The road was a mere lane, winding over bare swells of bleak and barren-looking land. The houses were few and far between, besides being small and rusty, though they appeared to be kept in good repair, and their door-yards, which were the unfenced Cape, were tidy; or, rather, they looked as if the ground around them was blown clean by the wind. Perhaps the scarcity of wood here, and the consequent absence of the wood-pile and other wooden traps, had something to do with this appearance. They seemed, like mariners ashore, to have sat right down to enjoy the firmness of the land, without studying their postures or habiliments. To them it was merely *terra firma* and *cognita*, not yet *fertilis* and *jucunda*. Every landscape which is dreary enough has a certain beauty to my eyes, and in this instance its permanent qualities were enhanced by the weather. Everything told of the sea, even when we did not see its waste or hear its roar. For birds there were gulls, and for carts in the fields, boats turned bottom upward against the houses, and sometimes the rib of a whale was woven into the fence by the roadside. The trees were, if possible, rarer than the houses, excepting apple-trees, of which there were a few small orchards in the hollows. These were either narrow and high, with flat tops, having lost their side branches, like huge plum-bushes growing in exposed situations, or else dwarfed and branching immediately at the ground, like quince-bushes. They suggested that, under like circumstances, all trees would at last acquire like habits of growth. I afterward saw on the Cape many full-grown apple-trees not higher than a man's head; one whole orchard, indeed, where all the fruit could have been gathered by a man standing on the ground; but you could hardly creep beneath the trees. . . .

The most foreign and picturesque structures on the Cape, to an inlander, not excepting the salt-works, are the wind-mills,—gray-looking, octagonal towers, with long timbers slanting to the ground in the rear, and there resting on a cart-wheel, by which their fans are turned round to face the wind. These appeared also to serve in some measure for props against its force. A great circular rut was worn around the building by the wheel. The neighbors who assemble to turn the mill to the wind are likely to know which way it blows, without a weathercock. They looked loose and slightly locomotive, like huge wounded birds, trailing a wing or a leg, and reminded one of pictures of the Netherlands. Being on elevated ground, and high in themselves, they serve as landmarks,—for there are no tall trees, or other objects commonly, which can be seen at a distance in the horizon; though the outline of the land itself is so firm and distinct, that an insignificant cone, or even precipice of sand, is visible at a great distance from over the sea. Sailors making the land commonly steer either by the wind-mills, or the meeting-houses. In the country, we are obliged to steer by the meeting-houses alone. Yet the meeting-house is a kind of wind-mill, which runs one day in seven, turned either by the winds of doctrine or public opinion, or more rarely by the winds of Heaven, where another sort of grist is ground, of which, if it be not all bran or musty, if it be not *plaster*, we trust to make bread of life. . . .

11. Shore of Crystal Pond, Orleans (11/19/03)

"This was a grand place to walk. There were two or three more of those peculiar ponds with high, shiny sand-banks, by which you detected them before you saw the water, as if freshly scooped out of the high plains or a table-land. . . ."

12. Old windmill (1797) from South Chatham (11/19/03)

THE PLAINS OF NAUSET

13. Distant view of old windmill with wreck in the foreground, Chatham (11/19/03)

Thoreau does not mention windmills in his Journal notes for his 1855 and 1857 trips, during which he went near or through Chatham. But he and Channing might well have walked past the old mill built in 1793, still noted on maps of Cape Cod, a little northwest of Eastham proper. T.W.

. . . The barren aspect of the land would hardly be believed if described. It was such soil, or rather land, as, to judge from appearances, no farmer in the interior would think of cultivating, or even fencing. Generally, the ploughed fields of the Cape look white and yellow, like a mixture of salt and Indian meal. This is called soil. All an inlander's notions of soil and fertility will be confounded by a visit to these parts, and he will not be able, for some time afterward, to distinguish soil from sand. . . .

"In 1667 the town [of Eastham] voted that every housekeeper should kill twelve blackbirds, or three crows, which did great damage to the corn, and this vote was repeated for many years." In 1695 an additional order was passed, namely, that "every unmarried man in the township shall kill six blackbirds, or three crows, while he remains single; as a penalty for not doing it, shall not be married until he obey this order. . . ."

It is sufficiently remarkable that any crops can be raised here, and it may be owing, as others have suggested, to the amount of moisture in the atmosphere, the warmth of the sand, and the rareness of frosts. A miller, who was sharpening his stones, told me that, forty years ago, he had been to a husking here, where five hundred bushels were husked in one evening, and the corn was piled six feet high or more, in the midst, but now, fifteen or eighteen bushels to an acre were an average yield. I never saw fields of such puny and unpromising-looking corn, as in this town. Probably the inhabitants are contented with small crops from a great surface easily cultivated. . . .

All the morning we had heard the sea roar on the eastern shore, which was several miles distant; for it still felt the effects of the storm in which the St. John was wrecked,—though a school-boy, whom we overtook, hardly knew what we meant, his ears were so used to it. He would have more plainly heard the same sound in a shell. It was a very inspiriting sound to walk by, filling the whole air, that of the sea dashing against the land, heard several miles inland. Instead of having a

14. Cape Cod farmhouse, Eastham (10/20/03)

The tree is gigantic compared to most of the ones Thoreau describes. T.W.

dog to growl before your door, to have an Atlantic Ocean to growl for a whole Cape! On the whole, we were glad of the storm, which would show us the ocean in its angriest mood. Charles Darwin was assured that the roar of the surf on the coast of Chiloe,* after a heavy gale, could be heard at night a distance of "21 sea miles across a hilly and wooded country." ... At length, before we got to Eastham meeting-house, we left the road and struck across the country for the eastern shore at Nauset Lights,—three lights close together, two or three miles distant from us. They were so many that they might be distinguished from others; but this seemed a shiftless and costly way of accomplishing that object. We found ourselves at once on an apparently boundless plain, without a tree or a fence, or, with one or two exceptions, a house in sight. Instead of fences, the earth was sometimes thrown up into a slight ridge. My companion compared it to the rolling prairies of Illinois. In the storm of wind and rain which raged when we traversed it, it no doubt appeared more vast and desolate than it really is. As there were no hills, but only here and there a dry hollow in the midst of the waste, and the distant horizon was concealed by mist, we did not know whether it was high or low. A solitary traveler, whom we saw perambulating in the distance, loomed like a giant. He appeared to walk slouchingly, as if held up from above by straps under his shoulders, as much as supported by the plain below. Men and boys would have appeared alike at a little distance, there being no object by which to measure them. Indeed, to an inlander, the Cape landscape is a constant mirage. This kind of country extended a mile or two each way. These were the "Plains of Nauset," once covered with wood, where in winter the winds howl and the snow blows right merrily in the face of the traveler. ...

At length we reached the seemingly retreating boundary of the plain, and entered what had appeared at a distance an upland marsh,

---

*Chile

15. Nauset Light from the south with beach grass in the foreground
(10/30/03)

A familiar sight, the edge of a dune, laced with beach grass that
stands out in fragile detail against the sky! T.W.

but proved to be dry sand covered with beach-grass, the bearberry, bayberry, shrub-oaks, and beach-plum, slightly ascending as we approached the shore; then, crossing over a belt of sand on which nothing grew, though the roar of the sea sounded scarcely louder than before, and we were prepared to go half a mile farther, we suddenly stood on the edge of a bluff overlooking the Atlantic. Far below us was the beach, from half a dozen to a dozen rods in width, with a long line of breakers rushing to the strand. The sea was exceedingly dark and stormy, the sky completely overcast, the clouds still dropping rain, and the wind seemed to blow not so much as the exciting cause, as from sympathy with the already agitated ocean. The waves broke on the bars at some distance from the shore, and curving green or yellow as if over so many unseen dams, ten or twelve feet high, like a thousand waterfalls, rolled in foam to the sand. There was nothing but that savage ocean between us and Europe.

Having got down the bank, and as close to the water as we could, where the sand was the hardest, leaving the Nauset Lights behind us, we began to walk leisurely up the beach, in a northwest direction, toward Provincetown, which was about twenty-five miles distant, still sailing under our umbrellas with a strong aft wind, admiring in silence, as we walked, the great force of the ocean stream,

The white breakers were rushing to the shore; the foam ran up the sand, and then ran back as far as we could see (and we imagined how much farther along the Atlantic coast, before and behind us), as regularly, to compare great things with small, as the master of a choir beats time with his white wand; and ever and anon a higher wave caused us hastily to deviate from our path, and we looked back on our tracks filled with water and foam. The breakers looked like droves of a thousand wild horses of Neptune, rushing to the shore, with their white manes streaming far behind; and when, at length, the sun shone for a moment, their manes were rainbow-tinted. Also, the long kelp-weed

16. Beach grass and poverty grass on Nauset Bluffs, Eastham (10/30/03)
Fall and winter storms pile sand high around these tufts, which sprout new shoots in the spring, year after year, until a solid ridge is formed with sufficient growth on it to hold the sand down. T.W.

was tossed up from time to time, like the tails of sea-cows sporting in the brine.

... The only human beings whom we saw on the beach for several days were one or two wreckers looking for drift-wood, and fragments of wrecked vessels.... We soon met one of these wreckers,—a regular Cape Cod man, with whom we parleyed, with a bleached and weather-beaten face, within whose wrinkles I distinguished no particular feature. It was like an old sail endowed with life,—a hanging-cliff of weather-beaten flesh,—like one of the clay boulders which occurred in that sand-bank. He had on a hat which had seen salt water, and a coat of many pieces and colors, though it was mainly the color of the beach, as if it had been sanded. His variegated back—for his coat had many patches, even between the shoulders—was a rich study to us when we had passed him and looked around. It might have been dishonorable for him to have so many scars behind, it is true, if he had not had many more and more serious ones in front.... He was looking for wrecks, old logs, water-logged and covered with barnacles, or bits of boards and joists, even chips which he drew out of the reach of the tide, and stacked up to dry. When the log was too large to carry far, he cut it up where the last wave had left it, or rolling it a few feet, appropriated it by sticking two sticks into the ground crosswise above it. Some rotten trunk, which in Maine cumbers the ground, and is, perchance, thrown into the water on purpose, is here thus carefully picked up, split and dried, and husbanded. Before winter the wrecker painfully carries these things up the bank on his shoulders by a long diagonal slanting path made with a hoe in the sand, if there is no hollow* at hand. You may see his hooked pike-staff always lying on the bank, ready for use. He is the true monarch of the beach, whose "right there is none to dispute," and he is as much identified with it as a beach-bird.

---

*A "hollow," such as Cahoon's Hollow, was worn into the bank by the action of the sea and often extended into a valley that sometimes cut across the Cape, at right angles to the ocean. T.W.

17. Nauset Lights from the north (10/20/03)

"...I thought of those summery hours when time is tinged with eternity,—runs into it and becomes of one stuff with it."

. . . The wrecker directed us to a slight depression, called Snow's Hollow, by which we ascended the bank,—for elsewhere, if not difficult, it was inconvenient to climb it on account of the sliding sand which filled our shoes.

This sandbank—the backbone of the Cape—rose directly from the beach to the height of a hundred feet or more above the ocean. It was with singular emotions that we first stood upon it and discovered what a place we had chosen to walk on. On our right, beneath us, was the beach of smooth and gently-sloping sand, a dozen rods in width; next, the endless series of white breakers; further still, the light green water over the bar, which runs the whole length of the fore-arm of the Cape, and beyond this stretched the unwearied and illimitable ocean. On our left, extending back from the very edge of the bank, was a perfect desert of shining sand, from thirty to eighty rods in width, skirted in the distance by small sand-hills fifteen or twenty feet high; between which, however, in some places, the sand penetrated as much farther. Next commenced the region of vegetation,—a succession of small hills and valleys covered with shrubbery, now glowing with the brightest imaginable autumnal tints; and beyond this were seen, here and there, the waters of the bay. Here, in Wellfleet, this pure sand plateau, known to sailors as the Table Lands of Eastham, on account of its appearance, as seen from the ocean, and because it once made a part of that town, —full fifty rods in width, and in many places much more, . . . stretched away northward from the southern boundary of the town, without a particle of vegetation. . . ; slightly rising towards the ocean, then stooping to the beach, by as steep a slope as sand could lie on, and as regular as a military engineer could desire. . . . From its surface we overlooked the greater part of the Cape. In short, we were traversing a desert with the view of an autumnal landscape of extraordinary brilliancy, a sort of Promised Land, on the one hand, and the ocean on the other. Yet, though the prospect was so extensive, and the country for the most part destitue of trees, a house was rarely visible,—we never saw one from the beach,—and the solitude was that of the ocean and the desert com-

18. Wellfleet Bluffs from Cahoon's Hollow (10/21/03)

Perhaps it was wrong to expect passages about the ocean in Thoreau's Journal after his Cape Cod trips. Water is so completely his element, the ocean no doubt became part of the force already in his being, not a separate entity in his thoughts. T.W.

bined. A thousand men could not have seriously interrupted it, but would have been lost in the vastness of the scenery as their footsteps in the sand.

. . . I was comparatively satisfied. There I had got the Cape under me, as much as if I were riding it barebacked. It was not as on the map or seen from the stage-coach; but there I found it all out of doors, huge and real, Cape Cod! . . .

We walked on quite at our leisure, now on the beach, now on the bank,—sitting from time to time on some damp log, maple or yellow birch, which had long followed the seas, but had now at last settled on land; or under the lee of a sand-hill, on the bank, that we might gaze steadily on the ocean. The bank was so steep, that, where there was no danger of its caving, we sat on its edge as on a bench. It was difficult for us landsmen to look out over the ocean without imagining land in the horizon; yet the clouds appeared to hang low over it, and rest on the water as they never do on the land, perhaps on account of the great distance to which we saw.

The sand was not without advantage, for, though it was "heavy" walking in it, it was soft to the feet; and, notwithstanding that it had been raining nearly two days, when it held up for half an hour, the sides of the sand-hills, which were porous and sliding, afforded a dry seat. All the aspects of this desert are beautiful, whether you behold it in fair weather or foul, or when the sun is just breaking out after a storm, and shining on its moist surface in the distance, it is so white, and pure, and level, and each slight inequality and track is so distinctly revealed; and when your eyes slide off this, they fall on the ocean. In summer the mackerel gulls—which here have their nests among the neighboring sand-hills—pursue the traveler anxiously, now and then diving close to his head with a squeak, and he may see them, like swallows, chase some crow which has been feeding on the beach, almost across the Cape.

19. Sunrise from Cahoon's Hollow (10/21/03)
   "The water shines with an inward light like a heaven on earth."

Though for some time I have not spoken of the roaring of the break-ers, and the ceaseless flux and reflux of the waves, yet they did not for a moment cease to dash and roar, with such a tumult that, if you had been there, you could scarcely have heard my voice the while; and they are dashing and roaring this very moment, though it may be with less din and violence, for there the sea never rests. We were wholly absorbed by this spectacle and tumult, and like Chryses, though in a different mood from him, we walked silent along the shore of the resounding sea.

There was but little weed cast up here, and that kelp chiefly, there being scarcely a rock for rock-weed to adhere to. Who has not had a vision from some vessel's deck, when he had still his land-legs on, of this great brown apron, drifting half upright, and quite submerged through the green water, clasping a stone or a deep-sea mussel in its unearthly fingers? I have seen it carrying a stone half as large as my head. We sometimes watched a mass of this cable-like weed, as it was tossed up on the crest of a breaker, waiting with interest to see it come in, as if there was some treasure buoyed up by it; but we were always surprised and disappointed at the insignificance of the mass which had attracted us. . . . This kelp, oar-weed, tangle, devil's apron, sole-leather, or ribbon-weed,—as various species are called,—appeared to us a singu-larly marine and fabulous product, a fit invention for Neptune to adorn his car with, or a freak of Proteus. All that is told of the sea has a fabulous sound to an inhabitant of the land, and all its products have a certain fabulous quality, as if they belonged to another planet, from seaweed to a sailor's yarn, or a fish story. In this element the animal and vegetable kingdoms meet and are strangely mingled. . . .

The beach was also strewn with beautiful sea-jellies, which the wreckers called Sun-squall, one of the lowest forms of animal life, some white, some wine-colored, and a foot in diameter. . . . What right has the sea to bear in its bosom such tender things as sea-jellies and mosses, when it had such a boisterous shore, that the stoutest fabrics are wrecked

20. Along the back shore at Wellfleet dunes (10/21/03)

I never tired of watching a wave form, the whitecaps mirrored in the curve of translucent greens or blues beneath, before they piled up on the shore in foaming masses, then spread out with a sibilant murmur across the sand. T.W.

against it? Strange that it should undertake to dandle such delicate children in its arm.... Before the land rose out of the ocean, and became *dry* land, chaos reigned; and between high and low water-mark, where she is partially disrobed and rising, a sort of chaos reigns still, which only anomalous creatures can inhabit. Mackerel-gulls were all the while flying over our heads and amid the breakers, sometimes two white ones pursuing a black one; quite at home in the storm, though they are as delicate organizations as sea-jellies and mosses; and we saw that they were adapted to their circumstances rather by their spirits than their bodies. Theirs must be an essentially wilder, that is less human, nature, than that of larks and robins. Their note was like the sound of some vibrating metal, and harmonized well with the scenery and the roar of the surf, as if one had rudely touched the strings of the lyre, which ever lies on the shore; a ragged shred of ocean music tossed aloft on the spray....

21. Wreck of the "Florida," Wellfleet beach (10/21/03)
    The "Florida" was reported arriving in Provincetown Harbor with a cargo of Barbadoes rum, to await orders, in June of 1893. T.W.

Having walked about eight miles since we struck the beach, and passed the boundary between Wellfleet and Truro, a stone post in the sand,—for even this sand comes under the jurisdiction of one town or another,—we turned inland over barren hills and valleys, whither the sea, for some reason, did not follow us, and, tracing up a Hollow, discovered two or three sober-looking houses within half a mile, uncommonly near the eastern coast. Their garrets were apparently so full of chambers, that their roofs could hardly lie down straight, and we did not doubt that there was room for us there. Houses near the sea are generally low and broad. These were a story and a half high; but if you merely counted the windows in their gable ends, you would think that there were many stories more, or, at any rate, that the half-story was the only one thought worthy of being illustrated. The great number of windows in the ends of the houses, and their irregularity in size and position, here and elsewhere on the Cape, struck us agreeably,—as if each of the various occupants who had their *cunabula* behind had punched a hole where his necessities required it, and according to his size and stature, without regard to outside effect. There were windows for the grown folks, and windows for the children,—three or four apiece; as a certain man had a large hole cut in his barn-door for the cat, and another smaller one for the kitten. Sometimes they were so low under the eaves that I thought they must have perforated the plate beam for another apartment, and I noticed some which were triangular, to fit that part more exactly. The ends of the houses had thus as many muzzles as a revolver, and, if the inhabitants have the same habit of staring out the windows that some of our neighbors have, a traveler must stand a small chance with them.

These houses were on the shores of a chain of ponds, seven in number, the source of a small stream called Herring River, which empties into the Bay. There are many Herring Rivers on the Cape; they will, perhaps, be more numerous than herrings soon. . . .

22. Old Ryder House, Truro (10/23/03)

Cape Cod houses always seem to hug the ground, like this one—or to swish a string of small buildings airily behind them, like a woman whose long gown trails behind her. T.W.

Our host* took pleasure in telling us the names of the ponds, most of which we could see from his windows, and making us repeat them after him, to see if we had got them right. They were Gull Pond, the largest and a very handsome one, clear and deep, and more than a mile in circumference, Newcomb's, Swett's, Slough, Horse-Leech, Round, and Herring Ponds, all connected at high water, if I do not mistake. The coast-surveyors had come to him for their names, and he told them of one which they had not detected. He said that they were not so high as formerly. There was an earthquake about four years before he was born, which cracked the pans of the ponds, which were of iron, and caused them to settle. I did not remember to have read of this. Innumerable gulls used to resort to them; but the large gulls were now very scarce, for, as he said, the English robbed their nests far in the north, where they breed. . . .

This was the merriest old man that we had ever seen, and one of the best preserved. His style of conversation was coarse and plain enough to have suited Rabelais. He would have made a good Panurge. Or rather he was a sober Silenus, and we were the boys Chromis and Mnasilus, who listened to his story.

> "Not by Hæmonian hills the Thracian bard,
> Nor awful Phœbus was on Pindus heard
> With deeper silence or with more regard."

There was a strange mingling of past and present in his conversation, for he had lived under King George, and might have remembered when Napoleon and the moderns generally were born. He said that one day, when the troubles between the Colonies and the mother country first broke out, as he, a boy of fifteen, was pitching hay out of

---

*John Young Newcomb, the "Wellfleet Oysterman," Thoreau's and Channing's host for the night, who lived in a house like the one pictured on the preceding page, and with whom Thoreau had a long and amusing conversation that he reports with gusto. T.W.

23. Herring Ponds, Wellfleet (10/21/03)

"From time to time, summer and winter and far inland, I call to mind that peculiar prolonged cry of the upland plover on the bare heaths of Truro in July, heard from sea to sea, though you cannot guess how far the bird may be, as if it were a characteristic sound of the Cape."

a cart, one Donne, an old Tory, who was talking with his father, a good Whig, said to him: "Why, Uncle Bill, you might as well undertake to pitch that pond into the ocean with a pitchfork, as for the Colonies to undertake to gain their independence." . . .

The sounds which the ocean makes must be very significant and interesting to those who live near it. When I was leaving the shore at this place the next summer,* and had got a quarter of a mile distant, ascending a hill, I was startled by a sudden, loud sound from the sea, as if a large steamer were letting off steam by the shore, so that I caught my breath and felt my blood run cold for an instant, and I turned about, expecting to see one of the Atlantic steamers thus far out of her course, but there was nothing unusual to be seen. There was a low bank at the entrance of the Hollow, between me and the ocean, and suspecting that I might have risen into another stratum of air in ascending the hill,—which had wafted to me only the ordinary roar of the sea,—I immediately descended again, to see if I lost hearing of it; but, without regard to my ascending or descending, it died away in a minute or two, and yet there was scarcely any wind all the while. The old man said that this was what they called the "rut," a peculiar roar of the sea before the wind changes, which, however, he could not account for. . . .

Old Josselyn, who came to New England in 1638, has it among his weather-signs, that "the resounding of the sea from the shore, and murmuring of the winds in the woods, without apparent wind, sheweth wind to follow."

Being on another part of the coast one night since this, I heard the roar of the surf a mile distant, and the inhabitants said it was a sign that the wind would work round east, and we should have rainy weather. The ocean was heaped up somewhere at the eastward, and this roar was occasioned by its effort to preserve its equilibrium, the

---

*Thoreau went back to the Cape, alone, in June 1850. T.W.

24. Across Nauset Bay towards sand dunes in Eastham (10/20/03)

wave reaching the shore before the wind. Also the captain of a packet between this country and England told me that he sometimes met with a wave on the Atlantic coming against the wind, perhaps in a calm sea, which indicated that at a distance the wind was blowing from an opposite quarter, but the undulation had traveled faster than it. Sailors tell of "tide-rips" and "ground-swells," which they suppose to have been occasioned by hurricanes and earthquakes, and to have traveled many hundred, and sometimes even two or three thousand miles.

Our way* to the high sand-bank, which I have described as extending all along the coast, led, as usual, through patches of bayberry bushes, which straggled into the sand. This, next to the shrub-oak, was perhaps the most common shrub thereabouts. I was much attracted by its odoriferous leaves and small gray berries which are clustered about the short twigs, just below the last year's growth. . . . From the abundance of berries still hanging on the bushes, we judged that the inhabitants did not generally collect them for tallow, though we had seen a piece in the house we had just left. I have since made some tallow myself. Holding a basket beneath the bare twigs in April, I rubbed them together between my hands and thus gathered about a quart in twenty minutes, to which were added enough to make three pints, and I might have gathered them much faster with a suitable rake and a large shallow basket.** They have little prominences like those of an orange all creased in tallow, which also fills the interstices down to the stone. The oily part rose to the top, making it look like a savory black broth, which smelled much like balm or other herb tea. You let it cool, then skim off the tallow from the surface, melt this again and strain it. I got about a quarter of a pound weight from my three pints,

---

*From the Wellfleet Oysterman's house. T.W.

**There were no fruit-bearing bayberry bushes in Concord, but Thoreau gathered these in New Bedford woods, while visiting his friend Daniel Ricketson, in April 1857. T.W.

25. Cape Cod bayberries (10/21/03)

It is lovely on a crisp fall day to collect a handful of these berries and rub them between your hands to get their delightful, penetrating scent; then put them in your pocket and forget them till another outing —it might be weeks, months later—when they are like a secret prize awaiting the thrust of your hand. T.W.

and more yet remained within the berries. A small portion cooled in the form of small flattish hemispheres, like crystallizations, the size of a kernel of corn (nuggets I called them as I picked them out from amid the berries). . . . If you get any pitch on your hands in the pine-woods you have only to rub some of these berries between your hands to start it off. But the ocean was the grand fact there, which made us forget both bayberries and men.

Still held on without a break, the inland barrens and shrubbery, the desert and the high sand-bank with its even slope, the broad white beach, the breakers, the green water on the bar, and the Atlantic Ocean; and we traversed with delight new reaches of the shore; we took another lesson in sea-horses' manes and sea-cows' tails, in sea-jellies and sea-clams, with our new-gained experience. The sea ran hardly less than the day before. It seemed with every wave to be subsiding, because such was our expectation, and yet when hours had elapsed we could see no difference. But there it was, balancing itself, the restless ocean by our side, lurching in its gait. Each wave left the sand all braided or woven, as it were with a coarse woof and warp, and a distinct raised edge to its rapid work. We made no haste, since we wished to see the ocean at our leisure, and indeed that soft sand was no place in which to be in a hurry, for one mile there was as good as two elsewhere. Besides, we were obliged frequently to empty our shoes of the sand which one took in in climbing or descending the bank. . . .

Objects on the beach, whether men or inanimate things, look not only exceedingly grotesque, but much larger and more wonderful than they actually are. Lately, when approaching the sea-shore several degrees south of this, I saw before me, seemingly half a mile distant, what appeared like bold and rugged cliffs on the beach, fifteen feet high, and whitened by the sun and waves; but after a few steps it proved to be low heaps of rags,—part of the cargo of a wrecked vessel,—scarcely more than a foot in height. Once also it was my business to go in search of the relics of a human body, mangled by sharks, which had

26. Surf rolling over sand ridge, Wellfleet (10/21/03)

"As I walked along close to the edge of the water, the sea oscillating like a pendulum before me and each billow flowing with a flat white foaming edge and a rounded outline up the sand, it reminded me of the white toes of blue-stockinged feet thrust forward from under the garments in an endless dance. It was a contra-dance to the shore. Some waves would flow unexpectedly high and fill my shoes with water before I was aware of it. It is very exciting for a while to walk where half the floor before you is thus incessantly fluctuating."

just been cast up, a week after a wreck, having got the direction from a light-house . . . I expected that I must look very narrowly to find so small an object, but the sandy beach, half a mile wide, and stretching farther than the eye could reach, was so perfectly smooth and bare, and the mirage toward the sea so magnifying, that when I was half a mile distant the insignificant sliver which marked the spot looked like a bleached spar, and the relics were as conspicuous as if they lay in state on that sandy plain, or a generation had labored to pile up their cairn there. Close at hand they were simply some bones with a little flesh adhering to them, in fact, only a slight inequality in the sweep of the shore. There was nothing at all remarkable about them, and they were singularly inoffensive both to the senses and the imagination. But as I stood there they grew more and more imposing. They were alone with the beach and the sea, whose hollow roar seemed addressed to them, and I was impressed as if there was an understanding between them and the ocean which necessarily left me out, with my snivelling sympathies. . . .

Sometimes we helped a wrecker turn over a larger log than usual, or we amused ourselves with rolling stones down the bank, but we rarely could make one reach the water, the beach was so soft and wide; or we bathed in some shallow within a bar, where the sea covered us with sand at every flux, though it was quite cold and windy. The ocean there is commonly but a tantalizing prospect in hot weather, for with all that water before you, there is, as we were afterward told, no bathing on the Atlantic side, on account of the undertow and the rumor of sharks. At the light-house both in Eastham and Truro, the only houses quite on the shore, they declared, the next year, that they would not bathe there "for any sum," for they sometimes saw the sharks tossed up and quiver for a moment on the sand. Others laughed at these stories, but perhaps they could afford to because they never bathed anywhere. . . .

27. Cahoon's Hollow Life Saving Station, Wellfleet (10/21/03)

I should add, however, that in July* we walked on the bank here a quarter of a mile parallel with a fish about six feet in length, possibly a shark, which was prowling slowly along within two rods of the shore. It was of a pale brown color, singularly film-like and indistinct in the water, as if all nature abetted this child of ocean, and showed many darker transverse bars or rings whenever it came to the surface. It is well known that different fishes even of the same species are colored by the water they inhabit. We saw it go into a little cove or bathing-tub, where we had just been bathing, where the water was only four or five feet deep at that time, and after exploring it go slowly out again; but we continued to bathe there, only observing first from the bank if the cove was preoccupied. We thought that the water was fuller of life, more aerated perhaps than that of the Bay, like soda-water, for we were as particular as young salmon, and the expectation of encountering a shark did not subtract anything from its life-giving qualities.

Sometimes we sat on the wet beach and watched the beach birds, sand-pipers, and others, trotting along close to each wave, and waiting for the sea to cast up their breakfast. The former (*Charadrius melodus*) ran with great rapidity, and then stood stock still, remarkably erect, and hardly to be distinguished from the beach. The wet sand was covered with small skipping Sea Fleas, which apparently made a part of their food. These last are the little scavengers of the beach, and are so numerous that they will devour large fishes, which have been cast up, in a very short time. One little bird not larger than a sparrow—it may have been a Phalarope—would alight on the turbulent surface where the breakers were five or six feet high, and float bouyantly there like a duck, cunningly taking to its wings and lifting itself a few feet through the air over the foaming crest of each breaker, but sometimes outriding safely a considerable billow which hid it some seconds, when its instinct told it that it would not break. It was a little creature thus

---

*Thoreau is referring to his third trip to the Cape, also made with Channing, in July 1855. T.W.

28. Highland Light from the south (10/21/03)

It was an awesome experience to watch the rays of the light, which seemed to end in soft rounded tips, sweep slowly around the country-side while the surf roard beneath the cliff. Somehow the *silence* of the huge revolving beams was surprising. T.W.

to sport with the ocean, but it was as perfect a success in its way as the breakers in theirs. . . .

Thus we kept on along the gently curving shore, seeing two or three miles ahead at once,—along this ocean sidewalk, where there was none to turn out for, with the middle of the road the highway of nations on our right, and the sand cliffs of the Cape on our left. . . .

The sea, vast and wild as it is, . . . lets nothing lie; not even the giant clams which cling to its bottom. It is still heaving up the tow-cloth of the Franklin, and perhaps a piece of some old pirate's ship, wrecked more than a hundred years ago, comes ashore to-day. Some years since, when a vessel was wrecked here which had nutmegs in her cargo, they were strewn all along the beach, and for a considerable time were not spoiled by the salt water. Soon afterward, a fisherman caught a cod which was full of them. Why, then, might not the Spice-Islanders shake their nutmeg-trees into the ocean, and let all nations who stand in need of them pick them up?

. . . I picked up a bottle half buried in the wet sand, covered with barnacles, but stoppled tight, and half full of red ale, which still smacked of juniper,—all that remained I fancied from the wreck of a rowdy world,—that great salt sea on the one hand, and this little sea of ale on the other, preserving their separate characters. What if it could tell us its adventures over countless ocean waves! Man would not be man through such ordeals as it had passed. But as I poured it slowly out on to the sand, it seemed to me that man himself was like a half-emptied bottle of pale ale, which Time had drunk so far, yet stoppled tight for a while, and drifting about in the ocean of circumstances, but destined erelong to mingle with the surrounding waves, or be spilled amid the sands of a distant shore. . . .

29. Sunrise from harbor, Chatham (10/20/03)

To-day it was the Purple Sea, an epithet which I should not before have accepted. There were distinct patches of the color of a purple grape with the bloom rubbed off. But first and last the sea is of all colors. . . . Commonly, in calm weather, for half a mile from the shore, where the bottom tinges it, the sea is green, or greenish, as are some ponds; then blue for many miles, often with purple tinges, bounded in the distance by a light, almost silvery stripe; beyond which there is generally a dark blue rim, like a mountain ridge in the horizon, as if, like that, it owed its color to the intervening atmosphere. On another day, it will be marked with long streaks, alternately smooth and rippled, light-colored and dark, even like our inland meadows in a freshet, and showing which way the wind sets.

Thus we sat on the foaming shore, looking on the wine-colored ocean,—

Θίν᾽ ἔφ᾽ ἁλὸς πολιῆς ὁρόων ἐπὶ οἴνοπα πόντον.

Here and there was a darker spot on its surface, the shadow of a cloud, though the sky was so clear that no cloud would have been noticed otherwise, and no shadow would have been seen on the land, where a much smaller surface is visible at once.

Though there were numerous vessels at this great distance in the horizon on every side, yet the vast spaces between them, like the spaces between the stars,—far as they were distant from us, so were they from one another—nay, some were twice as far from each other as from us,—impressed us with a sense of the immensity of the ocean, the "unfruit-ful ocean," as it has been called, and we could see what proportion man and his works bear to the globe. As we looked off, and saw the water growing darker and darker and deeper and deeper the farther we looked, till it was awful to consider, and it appeared to have no relation to the friendly land, either as shore or bottom,—of what use is a bottom if it is out of sight, if it is two or three miles from the sur-face, and you are to be drowned so long before you get to it, though it were made of the same stuff with your native soil?—over that ocean where, as the Veda says, "there is nothing to give support, nothing to rest upon, nothing to cling to," I felt that I was a land animal....

On Cape Cod the next most eastern land you hear of is St. George's Bank (the fishermen tell of "Georges," "Cashus," and other sunken lands which they frequent). Every Cape man has a theory about George's Bank having been an island once, and in their accounts they gradually reduce the shallowness from six, five, four, two fathoms, to somebody's confident assertion that he has seen a mackerel-gull sitting on a piece of dry land there. It reminded me, when I thought of the ship-wrecks which had taken place there, of the Isle of Demons, laid down off this coast in old charts of the New World. There must be something monstrous, methinks, in a vision of the sea bottom from over some bank a thousand miles from the shore, more awful than its imagined bottomlessness; a drowned continent, all livid and frothing at the nostrils, like the body of a drowned man, which is better sunk deep than near the surface.

The Greeks would not have called the ocean ἀτρύγετος, or unfruit-ful, though it does not produce wheat, if they had viewed it by the light of modern science, for naturalists now assert that "the sea, and not the land, is the principal seat of life,"... In short, the dry land itself came through and out of the water in its way to the heavens, for, "in going back through the geological ages, we come to an epoch when, according to all appearances, the dry land did not exist, and when the surface of our globe was entirely covered with water."* We looked on the sea, then, once more, not as ἀτρύγετος or unfruitful, but as it has been more truly called, the "laboratory of continents."

---

*Thoreau is here quoting Édouard Desor (1811–1882), Swiss geologist who col-laborated with Louis Agassiz (whom Thoreau also quotes earlier in the same passage) in his mountain and glacier researches. T.W.

. . . There were thin belts of wood in Wellfleet and Truro, a mile or more from the Atlantic, but, for the most part, we could see the horizon through them, or, if extensive, the trees were not large. Both oaks and pines had often the same flat look with the apple-trees. Commonly, the oak woods twenty-five years old were a mere scraggy shrubbery nine or ten feet high, and we could frequently reach to their topmost leaf. Much that is called "woods" was about half as high as this,—only patches of shrub-oak, bayberry, beach-plum, and wild roses, overrun with woodbine. When the roses were in bloom, these patches in the midst of the sand displayed such a profusion of blossoms, mingled with the aroma of the bayberry, that no Italian or other artificial rose-garden could equal them. They were perfectly Elysian, and realized my idea of an oasis in the desert. . . .

The inhabitants of these towns have a great regard for a tree, though their standard for one is necessarily neither large nor high; and when they tell you of the large trees that once grew here, you must think of them, not as absolutely large, but large compared with the present generation. Their "brave old oaks," of which they speak with so much respect, and which they will point out to you as relics of the primitive forest, one hundred or one hundred and fifty, ay, for aught they know, two hundred years old, have a ridiculously dwarfish appearance, which excites a smile in the beholder. The largest and most venerable which they will show you in such a case are, perhaps, not more than twenty or twenty-five feet high. I was especially amused by the Lilliputian old oaks in the south part of Truro. To the inexperienced eye, which appreciated their proportions only, they might appear vast as the tree which saved his royal majesty, but measured they were dwarfed at once almost into lichens which a deer might eat up in a morning. Yet they will tell you that large schooners were once built of timber which grew in Wellfleet. The old houses also are built of the timber of the Cape; but instead of the forests in the midst of which they originally stood, barren heaths, with poverty-grass for heather, now stretch away on every side. . . .

30. Apple tree, North Truro (10/23/03)

"... I measured some near the Highland Light in Truro, which had been taken from the shrubby woods thereabouts when young, and grafted. One, which had been set ten years, was on an average eighteen inches high, and spread nine feet, with a flat top. It had borne one bushel of apples two years before. Another, probably twenty years old from the seed, was five feet high, and spread eighteen feet, branching, as usual, at the ground, so that you could not creep under it. This bore a barrel of apples two years before. The owner of these trees invariably used the personal pronoun in speaking of them; as, 'I got *him* out of the woods, but *he* doesn't bear.' "

To-day we were walking through Truro, a town of about eighteen hundred inhabitants. We had already come to Pamet River, which empties into the Bay. This was the limit of the Pilgrims' journey up the Cape from Provincetown, when seeking a place for settlement. It rises in a hollow within a few rods of the Atlantic, and one who lives near its source told us that in high tides the sea leaked through, yet the wind and waves preserve intact the barrier between them, and thus the whole river is steadily driven westward butt-end foremost,— fountain-head, channel, and light-house, at the mouth, all together.

Early in the afternoon we reached the Highland Light, whose white tower we had seen rising out of the bank in front of us for the last mile or two. It is fourteen miles from the Nauset Lights, on what is called the Clay pounds, an immense bed of clay abutting on the Atlantic, and, as the keeper told us, stretching quite across the Cape, which is here only about two miles wide. We perceived at once a difference in the soil, for there was an interruption of the desert, and a slight appearance of a sod under our feet, such as we had not seen for the last two days.

31. Truro, looking across Pamet River at high tide (10/23/03)
   ". . . The boundaries of the actual are not more fixed and rigid than
the elasticity of our imagination. . . ."

After arranging to lodge at the light-house,* we rambled across the Cape to the Bay, over a singularly bleak and barren-looking country, consisting of rounded hills and hollows, called by geologists diluvial elevations and depressions,—a kind of scenery which has been compared to a chopped sea, though this suggests too sudden a transition. There is a delineation of this very landscape in Hitchcock's Report on the Geology of Massachusetts, a work which, by its size at least, reminds one of a diluvial elevation itself. Looking southward from the light-house, the Cape appeared like an elevated plateau, sloping very regularly, though slightly, downward from the edge of the bank on the Atlantic side, about one hundred and fifty feet above the ocean, to that on the Bay side. On traversing this we found it to be interrupted by broad valleys or gullies, which become the hollows in the bank when the sea has worn up to them. They are commonly at right angles with the shore, and often extend quite across the Cape.

---

*That is, in the home of the light-house keeper, Mr. Small. T.W.

32. Old fish house, Pleasant Bay, South Orleans (11/19/03)

Some of the valleys, however, are circular, a hundred feet deep, without any outlet, as if the Cape had sunk in those places, or its sands had run out. The few scattered houses which we passed, being placed at the bottom of the hollows, for shelter and fertility, were, for the most part, concealed entirely, as much as if they had been swallowed up in the earth. Even a village with its meeting-house, which we had left little more than a stone's throw behind, had sunk into the earth, spire and all, and we saw only the surface of the upland and the sea on either hand. When approaching it, we had mistaken the belfry for a summer-house on the plain. We began to think that we might tumble into a village before we were aware of it, as into an ant-lion's hole, and be drawn into the sand irrecoverably. The most conspicuous objects on the land were a distant windmill, or a meeting-house standing alone, for only they could afford to occupy an exposed place. A great part of the township, however, is a barren, heath-like plain, and perhaps one third of it lies in common, though the property of individuals.

33. Cranberry Bog, near Wellfleet Bluffs (11/19/03)

An example of one of the "circular valleys" Thoreau describes. It might just as well have contained a village instead of a bog. Before the advent of sandmobiles, one could find a small pocket in the dunes and spend a whole day in complete privacy. T.W.

This peculiar open country, with here and there a patch of shrubbery, extends as much as seven miles, or from Pamet River on the south
to High Head on the north, and from Ocean to Bay. To walk over
it makes on a stranger such an impression as being at sea, and he finds
it impossible to estimate distances in any weather. A windfall or a
herd of cows may seem to be far away in the horizon, yet, after going
a few rods, he will be close upon them. He is also deluded by other
kinds of mirage. When, in the summer, I saw a family a-blueberrying
a mile off, walking about amid the dwarfish bushes which did not come
up higher than their ankles, they seemed to me to be a race of giants,
twenty feet high at least.

34. Bay of Cape Cod, north of North Truro (10/23/03)

"At East Harbor River, as I sat on the Truro end of the bridge, I saw a great flock of mackerel gulls, one hundred at least, on a sandy point, whitening the shore there like so many white stones... and uttering all together their vibrating shrill note."

The highest and sandiest portion next the Atlantic was thinly covered with beach-grass and indigo-weed. Next to this the surface of the upland generally consisted of white sand and gravel, like coarse salt, through which a scanty vegetation found its way up. . . . On a few hillsides the savory-leaved aster and mouse-ear alone made quite a dense sward, said to be very pretty when the aster is in bloom. In some parts the two species of poverty-grass *(Hudsonia tomentosa* and *ericoides),* which deserve a better name, reign for miles in little hemispherical tufts or islets, like moss, scattered over the waste. They linger in bloom there till the middle of July. Occasionally near the beach these rounded beds, as also those of the sea-sandwort *(Honkenya peploides),* were filled with sand within an inch of their tops, and were hard, like large ant-hills, while the surrounding sand was soft. In summer, if the poverty-grass grows at the head of a Hollow looking toward the sea, in a bleak position where the wind rushes up, the northern or exposed half of the tuft is sometimes all black and dead like an oven-broom, while the opposite half is yellow with blossoms, the whole hillside thus presenting a remarkable contrast when seen from the poverty-stricken and the flourishing side. This plant, which in many places would be esteemed an ornament, is here despised by many on account of its being associated with barrenness.

The single road which runs lengthwise the Cape, now winding over the plain, now through the shrubbery which scrapes the wheels of the stage, was a mere cart-track, in the sand, commonly without any fences to confine it, and continually changing from this side to that, to harder ground, or sometimes to avoid the tide. But the inhabitants travel the waste here and there pilgrim-wise and staff in hand, by narrow footpaths, through which the sand flows out and reveals the nakedness of the land. We shuddered at the thought of living there and taking our afternoon walks over those barren swells, where we could overlook every step of our walk before taking it, and would have to pray for a fog or a snow-storm to conceal our destiny. The walker there must soon eat his heart.

35. Poverty grass (10/23/03)

"Is it not as language that all natural objects affect the poet? He sees a flower or other object, and it is beautiful or affecting to him because it is a symbol of his thought, and what he indistinctly feels or perceives is matured in some other organization. The objects I behold correspond to my mood."

In the north part of the town there is no house from shore to shore for several miles, and it is as wild and solitary as the Western Prairies— used to be. Indeed, one who has seen every house in Truro, will be surprised to hear of the number of the inhabitants, but perhaps five hundred of the men and boys of this small town were then abroad on their fishing-grounds. Only a few men stay at home to till the sand or watch for blackfish. The farmers are fishermen-farmers and understand better ploughing the sea than the land. They do not disturb their sands much, though there is a plenty of sea-weed in the creeks, to say nothing of blackfish occasionally rotting on the shore. Between the Pond and East Harbor Village there was an interesting plantation of pitch-pines, twenty or thirty acres in extent, like those which we had already seen from the stage. One who lived near said that the land was purchased by two men for a shilling or twenty-five cents an acre. Some is not considered worth writing a deed for. This soil or sand, which was partially covered with poverty and beach grass, sorrel, etc., was furrowed at intervals of about four feet and the seed dropped by a machine. The pines had come up admirably and grown the first year three or four inches, and the second six inches and more. Where the seed had been lately planted the white sand was freshly exposed in an endless furrow winding round and round the sides of the deep hollows in a vortical, spiral manner, which produced a very singular effect, as if you were looking into the reverse side of a vast banded shield. This experiment, so important to the Cape, appeared very successful, and perhaps the time will come when the greater part of this kind of land in Barnstable County will be thus covered with an artificial pine-forest, as has been done in some parts of France. . . .

The objects around us, the makeshifts of fishermen ashore, often made us look down to see if we were standing on terra firma. In the wells everywhere a block and tackle were used to raise the bucket, instead of a windlass, and by almost every house was laid up a spar or a plank or two full of auger-holes, saved from a wreck. The windmills

36. Pitch-pine plantation, North Truro (10/23/03)

"About noon it cleared up and after dinner I set out for Province-town, straight across the country to the Bay where the new road strikes it, directly through the pine plantation, about one mile from the light-house . . . This part of Truro affords singularly interesting and cheering walks for me, with regular hollows or dimples shutting out the sea as completely as if in the midst of the continent, though when you stand on the plain you commonly see the sails of vessels standing up or down the coast on each side of you . . . I sat down on the boundless level and enjoyed the solitude, drank it in, the medicine for which I had pined. . ."

were partly built of these, and they were worked into the public bridges. The light-house keeper, who was having his barn shingled, told me casually that he had made three thousand good shingles for that purpose out of a mast. You would sometimes see an old oar used for a rail. Frequently also some fair-weather finery ripped off a vessel by a storm near the coast was nailed up against an outhouse. I saw fastened to a shed near the light-house a long new sign with the words "ANGLO SAXON" on it in large gilt letters, as if it were a useless part which the ship could afford to lose, or which the sailors had discharged at the same time with the pilot. But it interested somewhat as if it had been a part of the Argo, clipped off in passing through the Symplegades.

To the fisherman, the Cape itself is a sort of store-ship laden with supplies,—a safer and larger craft which carries the women and children, the old men and the sick, and indeed sea-phrases are as common on it as on board the vessel. Thus is it ever with a sea-going people. The old Northmen used to speak of the "keel-ridge" of the country, that is, the ridge of the Doffrafield Mountains, as if the land were a boat turned bottom up. I was frequently reminded of the Northmen here. The inhabitants of the Cape are often at once farmers and sea-rovers; they are more than vikings or kings of the bays, for their sway extends over the open sea also. A farmer in Wellfleet, at whose house I afterward spent a night, who had raised fifty bushels of potatoes the previous year, which is a large crop for the Cape, and had extensive salt-works, pointed to his schooner, which lay in sight, in which he and his man and boy occasionally ran down the coast a-trading as far as the Capes of Virginia. This was his market-cart, and his hired man knew how to steer her. Thus he drove two teams a-field,

> "ere the high *seas* appeared
> Under the opening eyelids of the morn."

Though probably he would not hear much of the "gray-fly" on his way to Virginia.

A great proportion of the inhabitants of the Cape are always thus

37. Sunrise over North Truro (10/23/03) [The building to the left with the elevated structure ascending from the pond was an icehouse. T.W.]

"There is something serenely glorious and memorable to me in the sight of the first cool sunlight.... The subdued light and the repose remind me of Hades...."

abroad about their teaming on some ocean highway or other, and the history of one of their ordinary trips would cast the Argonautic expedition into the shade. I have just heard of a Cape Cod captain who was expected home in the beginning of the winter from the West Indies, but was long since given up for lost, till his relations at length have heard with joy, that, after getting within forty miles of Cape Cod light, he was driven back by nine successive gales to Key West, between Florida and Cuba, and was once again shaping his course for home. Thus he spent his winter. In ancient times the adventures of these two or three men and boys would have been made the basis of a myth, but now such tales are crowded into a line of shorthand signs, like an algebraic formula in the shipping news. . . .

On our way back to the light-house, by whose whitewashed tower we steered as securely as the mariner by its light at night, we passed through a graveyard, which apparently was saved from being blown away by its slates, for they had enabled a thick bed of huckleberry bushes to root themselves amid the graves. We thought it would be worth the while to read the epitaphs where so many were lost at sea; however, as not only their lives, but commonly their bodies also, were lost or not identified, there were fewer epitaphs of this sort than we expected, though there were not a few. Their graveyard is the ocean. . . .

We read that the Clay pounds were so called, "because vessels have had the misfortune to be pounded against it in gales of wind," which we regard as a doubtful derivation. There are small ponds here, upheld by the clay, which were formerly called the Clay Pits. Perhaps this, or Clay Ponds, is the origin of the name. Water is found in the clay quite near the surface; but we heard of one man who had sunk a well in the sand close by, "till he could see stars at noonday," without finding any. Over this bare Highland the wind has full sweep. Even in July it blows the wings over the heads of the young turkeys, which do not know enough to head against it; and in gales the doors and windows are blown in, and you must hold on to the light-house to prevent being blown into the Atlantic. . . .

38. The Clay pounds at Highland Light, from the north (10/23/03)

An eclipse of the sun took place one summer while I was in Provincetown. A crowd gathered at Highland Light to witness it. (A few dove underwater at the instant of the eclipse to see how it looked from beneath the surface.) The changes of light and colors on the hills and valleys of Truro turned them into another eerie world. I was lost in it —until awakened by a sound as puny as the barking of a terrier against the sea. People were *clapping their hands* at the spectacle, as though it were some theatre performance for their special benefit. I can imagine the comments Thoreau would have made! T.W.

It was said in 1794 that more vessels were cast away on the east shore of Truro than anywhere in Barnstable County. Notwithstanding that this light-house has since been erected, after almost every storm we read of one or more vessels wrecked here, and sometimes more than a dozen wrecks are visible from this point at one time. The inhabitants hear the crash of vessels going to pieces as they sit round their hearths, and they commonly date from some memorable shipwreck. If the history of this beach could be written from beginning to end, it would be a thrilling page in the history of commerce.

Truro was settled in the year 1700 as *Dangerfield*. This was a very appropriate name, for I afterward read on a monument in the grave-yard, near Pamet River, the following inscription:—

> Sacred
> to the memory of
> 57 citizens of Truro,
> who were lost in seven
> vessels, which
> foundered at sea in
> the memorable gale
> of Oct. 3d, 1841.

Their names and ages by families were recorded on different sides of the stone. They are said to have been lost on George's Bank, and I was told that only one vessel drifted ashore on the back side of the Cape, with the boys locked into the cabin and drowned. It is said that the homes of all were "within a circuit of two miles." Twenty-eight inhabitants of Dennis were lost in the same gale; and I read that "in one day, immediately after this storm, nearly or quite one hundred bodies were taken up and buried on Cape Cod." The Truro Insurance Company failed for want of skippers to take charge of its vessels. But the surviving inhabitants went a-fishing again the next year as usual. I found that it would not do to speak of shipwrecks there, for almost every family has lost some of its members at sea. "Who lives in that house?" I inquired. "Three widows," was the reply. . . .

39. Truro Memorial (10/23/03)

The Highland Light-house,* where we were staying, is a substantial-looking building of brick, painted white, and surmounted by an iron cap. Attached to it is the dwelling of the keeper, one story high, also of brick, and built by government. As we were going to spend the night in a light-house, we wished to make the most of so novel an experience, and therefore told our host that we would like to accompany him when he went to light up. At rather early candle-light he lighted a small Japan lamp, allowing it to smoke rather more than we like on ordinary occasions, and told us to follow him. He led the way first through his bedroom, which was placed nearest to the light-house, and then through a long, narrow, covered passage-way, between white-washed walls like a prison entry, into the lower part of the light-house, where many great butts of oil were arranged around; thence we ascended by a winding and open iron stairway, with a steadily increasing scent of oil and lamp-smoke, to a trap-door in an iron floor, and through this into the lantern. It was a neat building, with everything in apple-pie order, and no danger of anything rusting there for want of oil. The light consisted of fifteen argand lamps, placed within smooth concave reflectors twenty-one inches in diameter, and arranged in two horizontal circles one above the other, facing every way excepting directly down the Cape. These were surrounded, at a distance of two or three feet, by large plate-glass windows, which defied the storms, with iron sashes, on which rested the iron cap. All the iron work, except the floor, was painted white. And thus the light-house was completed. . . .

*The light-house has since been rebuilt, and shows a *Fresnel* light. Thoreau [It was rebuilt in 1857. T.W.]

40. Highland Light, near view from the east (10/23/03)

I well remember our visits to these crisp white buildings. Like as not, we'd be invited to the kitchen for a piece of pie. The members of the crew often stopped at our shack for a chat on their rounds, and we learned much about Cape customs and colloquialisms from them: their way of accenting certain words, for example: "in the winter*time*," or of pronouncing "no'theaster" for nor'easter; and some of their stories of wrecks and rescues that were legend then. T.W.

It was even more cold and windy to-day than before, and we were frequently glad to take shelter behind a sand-hill. None of the elements were resting. On the beach there is a ceaseless activity, always something going on, in storm and in calm, winter and summer, night and day. Even the sedentary man here enjoys a breadth of view which is almost equivalent to motion. In clear weather the laziest may look across the Bay as far as Plymouth at a glance, or over the Atlantic as far as human vision reaches, merely raising his eyelids; or if he is too lazy to look after all, he can hardly help *hearing* the ceaseless dash and roar of the breakers. The restless ocean may at any moment cast up a whale or a wrecked vessel at your feet. All the reporters in the world, the most rapid stenographers, could not report the news it brings. No creature could move slowly where there was so much life around. The few wreckers were either going or coming, and the ships and the sand-pipers, and the screaming gulls overhead; nothing stood still but the shore. The little beach-birds trotted past close to the water's edge, or paused but an instant to swallow their food, keeping time with the elements. I wondered how they ever got used to the sea, that they ventured so near the waves. . . .

The seashore is a sort of neutral ground, a most advantageous point from which to contemplate this world. It is even a trivial place. The waves forever rolling to the land are too far-traveled and untamable to be familiar. Creeping along the endless beach amid the sun-squall and the foam, it occurs to us that we, too, are the product of sea-slime.

It is a wild, rank place, and there is no flattery in it. Strewn with crabs, horse-shoes, and razor-clams, and whatever the sea casts up,—a vast *morgue,* where famished dogs may range in packs, and crows come daily to glean the pittance which the tide leaves them. The carcasses of men and beasts together lie stately up upon its shelf, rotting and bleaching in the sun and waves, and each tide turns them in their beds, and tucks fresh sand under them. There is naked Nature,—inhumanly

41. Up the beach along the Truro shore (10/23/03)

Sometime, in the fog, this beach took on a quality of sizelessness, and the tide coming in against it sounded like a giant sifting pebbles. You walked as though in a cottony nowhere, now and then brought to reality by a specially high wave that reached out to grasp your feet. T.W.

sincere, wasting no thought on man, nibbling at the cliffy shore where gulls wheel amid the spray.

Though once there were more whales cast up here, I think that it was never more wild than now. We do not associate the idea of antiquity with the ocean, nor wonder how it looked a thousand years ago, as we do of the land, for it was equally wild and unfathomable always. The Indians have left no traces on its surface, but it is the same to the civilized man and the savage. The aspect of the shore only has changed. The ocean is a wilderness reaching round the globe, wilder than a Bengal jungle, and fuller of monsters, washing the very wharves of our cities and the gardens of our seaside residences. Serpents, bears, hyenas, tigers, rapidly vanish as civilization advances, but the most populous and civilized city cannot scare a shark far from its wharves. It is no further advanced than Singapore, with its tigers, in this respect. The Boston papers had never told me that there were seals in the harbor. I had always associated these with the Esquimaux and other outlandish people. Yet from the parlor windows along the coast you may see families of them sporting on the flats. They were as strange to me as the merman would be. . . .

Before sunset, having already seen the mackerel fleet returning into the Bay, we left the seashore on the north of Provincetown, and made our way across the desert to the eastern extremity of the town. From the first high sand-hill, covered with beach-grass and bushes to its top, on the edge of the desert, we overlooked the shrubby hill and swamp country which surrounds Provincetown on the north, and protects it, in some measure, from the invading sand. Notwithstanding the universal barrenness, and the contiguity of the desert, I never saw an autumnal landscape so beautifully painted as this was. It was like the richest rug imaginable spread over an uneven surface; no damask nor velvet, nor Tyrian dye or stuffs, nor the work of any loom, could ever

42. Shells found on the beach [these were at Harwich] (11/20/03)

"We must not expect to probe with our fingers the sanctuary of any life, whether animal or vegetable. If we do, we shall discover nothing but surface still ... The cause and the effect are equally evanescent and intangible. ..."

match it. There was the incredibly bright red of the Huckleberry, and the reddish brown of the Bayberry, mingled with the bright and living green of small Pitch-Pines, and also the duller green of the Bayberry, Boxberry, and Plum, the yellowish green of the Shrub-Oaks, and the various golden and yellow and fawn-colored tints of the Birch and Maple and Aspen,—each making its own figure, and, in the midst, the few yellow sandslides on the sides of the hills looked like the white floor seen through rents in the rug. Coming from the country as I did, and many autumnal woods as I had seen, this was perhaps the most novel and remarkable sight that I saw on the Cape. Probably the brightness of the tints was enhanced by contrast with the sand which surrounded this tract. This was a part of the furniture of Cape Cod. We had for days walked up the long and bleak piazza which runs along her Atlantic side, then over the sanded floor of her halls, and now we were being introduced into her boudoir. The hundred white sails crowding round Long Point into Provincetown Harbor, seen over the painted hills in front, looked like toy ships upon a mantel-piece.

The peculiarity of this autumnal landscape consisted in the lowness and thickness of the shrubbery, no less than in the brightness of the tints. It was like a thick stuff of worsted or a fleece, and looked as if a giant could take it up by the hem, or rather the tasseled fringe which trailed out on the sand, and shake it, though it needed not to be shaken. But no doubt the dust would fly in that case, for not a little has accumulated underneath it. Was it not such an autumnal landscape as this which suggested our high-colored rugs and carpets? Hereafter when I look on a richer rug than usual, and study its figures, I shall think, there are the huckleberry hills, and there the denser swamps of boxberry and blueberry; there the shrub-oak patches and the bayberries, there the maples and the birches and the pines. . . .

After threading a swamp full of boxberry, and climbing several hills covered with shrub-oaks, without a path, where shipwrecked men

43. From Telegraph Hill, Provincetown, toward Manomet (10/22/03)
[That is, looking due northwest across Cape Cod Bay to the outer
coastline of Plymouth Bay. T.W.]

would be in danger of perishing in the night, we came down upon the eastern extremity of the four planks which run the whole length of Provincetown street. This, which is the last town on the Cape, lies mainly in one street along the curving beach fronting the southeast. The sand-hills, covered with shrubbery and interposed with swamps and ponds, rose immediately behind it in the form of a crescent, which is from half a mile to a mile or more wide in the middle, and beyond these is the desert, which is the greater part of its territory, stretching to the sea on the east and west and north. The town is compactly built in the narrow space, from ten to fifty rods deep, between the harbor and the sand-hills, and contained at that time about twenty-six hundred inhabitants. The houses, in which a more modern and pretending style has at length prevailed over the fisherman's hut, stand on the inner or plank side of the street, and the fish and store houses, with the picturesque-looking windmills of the Salt-works, on the water side. The narrow portion of the beach between forming the street, about eighteen feet wide, the only one where one carriage could pass another, if there was more than one carriage in the town, looked much "heavier" than any portion of the beach or the desert which we had walked on, it being above the reach of the highest tide, and the sand being kept loose by the occasional passage of a traveler. We learned that the four planks on which we were walking had been bought by the town's share of the Surplus Revenue, the disposition of which was a bone of contention between the inhabitants, till they wisely resolved thus to put it under foot.

44. Street view in Provincetown (10/22/03)

For me this town was a new experience—the warm, small-town friendliness that I had never known before. In the winter one came to know all segments of society there: artists, fishermen, boatbuilders, store clerks. There were two men in particular, both dead now, who were my source of Provincetown color. One was a genial round-faced and round-bellied fisherman who used to sport a derby hat and bright red sweater. I can still hear his warm guttural drawl: "Listen to the gawd-damn fool rave!" And the "gawd-damn fool" was his boon companion, small, thin as a rail, and perpetually quivering with argument. "When my for'ead is shrinkled up tauter'n hell," he used to say, "I know I'm drunk." T.W.

... This was the most completely maritime town that we were ever in. It was merely a good harbor, surrounded by land, dry if not firm,—an inhabited beach, whereon fishermen cured and stored their fish, without any back country. When ashore the inhabitants still walk on planks. A few small patches have been reclaimed from the swamps, containing commonly half a dozen square rods only each. We saw one which was fenced with four lengths of rail; also a fence made wholly of hogshead staves stuck in the ground. These, and such as these, were all the cultivated and cultivable land in Provincetown. We were told that there were thirty or forty acres in all, but we did not discover a quarter part so much, and that was well dusted with sand, and looked as if the desert was claiming it. They are now turning some of their swamps into Cranberry Meadows on quite an extensive scale.

Yet far from being out of the way, Provincetown is directly in the way of the navigator, and he is lucky who does not run afoul of it in the dark. It is situated on one of the highways of commerce, and men from all parts of the globe touch there in the course of a year.

The mackerel fleet had nearly all got in before us, it being Saturday night, excepting that division which had stood down towards Chatham in the morning; and from a hill where we went to see the sun set in the Bay, we counted two hundred goodly looking schooners at anchor in the harbor at various distances from the shore, and more were yet coming round the Cape. As each came to anchor, it took in sail and swung round in the wind, and lowered its boat. They belong chiefly to Wellfleet, Truro, and Cape Ann. This was that city of canvas which we had seen hull down in the horizon. Near at hand, and under bare poles, they were unexpectedly black-looking vessels, μέλαιναι νῆες. A fisherman told us that there were fifteen hundred vessels in the mackerel fleet, and that he had counted three hundred and fifty in Provincetown Harbor at one time. Being obliged to anchor at a considerable distance from the shore on account of the shallowness of the water, they made

45. Fish wharf with flakes, Provincetown (10/22/03)

Whenever we felt like eating fish, it was a simple matter, at the signalling sound of gulls shrieking in the wake of a returning vessel, to go down to the dock and ask for some whiting—in those days worth nothing, but still the most delicate fish you can imagine. T.W.

the impression of a larger fleet than the vessels at the wharves of a large city. As they had been manœuvring out there all day seemingly for our entertainment, while we were walking northwestward along the Atlantic, so now we found them flocking into Provincetown Harbor at night, just as we arrived, as if to meet us, and exhibit themselves close at hand. Standing by Race Point and Long Point with various speed, they reminded me of fowls coming home to roost. . . .

The next morning, though it was still more cold and blustering than the day before, we took to the deserts again, for we spent our days wholly out of doors, in the sun when there was any, and in the wind which never failed. After threading the shrubby hill-country at the southwest end of the town, west of the Shank-Painter Swamp, whose expressive name—for we understood it at first as a landsman naturally would—gave it importance in our eyes, we crossed the sands to the shore south of Race Point and three miles distant, and thence roamed round eastward through the desert to where we had left the sea the evening before. We traveled five or six miles after we got out there, on a curving line, and might have gone nine or ten, over vast platters of pure sand, from the midst of which we could not see a particle of vegetation, excepting the distant thin fields of beach-grass, which crowned and made the ridges toward which the sand sloped upward on each side;—all the while in the face of a cutting wind as cold as January. . . .

In Dwight's Travels in New England it is stated that the inhabitants of Truro were formerly regularly warned under the authority of law in the month of April yearly, to plant beach-grass, as elsewhere they are warned to repair the highways. They dug up the grass in bunches, which were afterward divided into several smaller ones, and set about three feet apart, in rows, so arranged as to break joints and obstruct the passage of the wind. It spread itself rapidly, the weight of the seeds when ripe bending the heads of the grass, and so dropping directly by its side and vegetating there. In this way, for instance, they built up

46. Shank-Painter Swamps, Provincetown (10/22/03)

"It [Thoreau was speaking of phosphorescent wood] suggested to me how unexplored still are the realms of nature, that what we know and have seen is always an insignificant portion. We may any day take a walk as strange as Dante's imaginary one to L'Inferno or Paradiso."

again that part of the Cape between Truro and Provincetown where the sea broke over in the last century. . . .

Thus Cape Cod is anchored to the heavens, as it were, by a myriad little cables of beach-grass, and, if they should fail, would become a total wreck, and erelong go to the bottom. Formerly, the cows were permitted to go at large, and they ate many strands of the cable by which the Cape is moored, and well-nigh set it adrift, as the bull did the boat which was moored with a grass rope; but now they are not permitted to wander.

Provincetown was apparently what is called a flourishing town. Some of the inhabitants asked me if I did not think that they appeared to be well off generally. I said that I did, and asked how many there were in the almshouse. "Oh, only one or two, infirm or idiotic," answered they. The outward aspect of the houses and shops frequently suggested a poverty which their interior comfort and even richness disproved. You might meet a lady daintily dressed in the Sabbath morning, wading in among the sand-hills, from church, where there appeared no house fit to receive her, yet no doubt the interior of the house answered to the exterior of the lady. As for the interior of the inhabitants I am still in the dark about it. I had a little intercourse with some whom I met in the street, and was often agreeably disappointed by discovering the intelligence of rough, and what would be considered unpromising, specimens. . . .

47. Provincetown as it looks from the end of steamboat wharf
(10/22/03)

    On foggy days, the town was enveloped in pensive sounds. A lonely bell-buoy, a mile from shore, and a high-toned seamew from behind the town would take turns and sound so quickly, though gently, one upon the other, that their overtones never ceased. T.W.

... We took our seat upon the highest sand-hill overlooking the town, in mid-air, on a long plank stretched across between two hillocks of sand, where some boys were endeavoring in vain to fly their kite; and there we remained the rest of that forenoon looking out over the placid harbor, and watching for the first appearance of the steamer from Wellfleet, that we might be in readiness to go on board when we heard the whistle off Long Point.

We got what we could out of the boys in the mean while. Province-town boys are of course all sailors and have sailors' eyes. When we were at the Highland Light the last summer, seven or eight miles from Provincetown Harbor, and wished to know one Sunday morning if the Olata, a well-known yacht, had got in from Boston, so that we could return in her, a Provincetown boy about ten years old, who chanced to be at the table, remarked that she had. I asked him how he knew. "I just saw her come in," said he. When I expressed surprise that he could distinguish her from other vessels so far, he said that there were not so many of those two-topsail schooners about but that he could tell her. Palfrey* said, in his oration at Barnstable, the duck does not take to the water with a surer instinct than the Barnstable boy. [He might have said the Cape Cod boy as well.] He leaps from his leading-strings into the shrouds, it is but a bound from the mother's lap to the mast-head. He boxes the compass in his infant soliloquies. He can hand, reef, and steer by the time he flies a kite.

---

*Thoreau is here referring to John Gorham Palfrey (1796–1881), American Unitarian clergyman and historian, as well as sometimes politician. T.W.

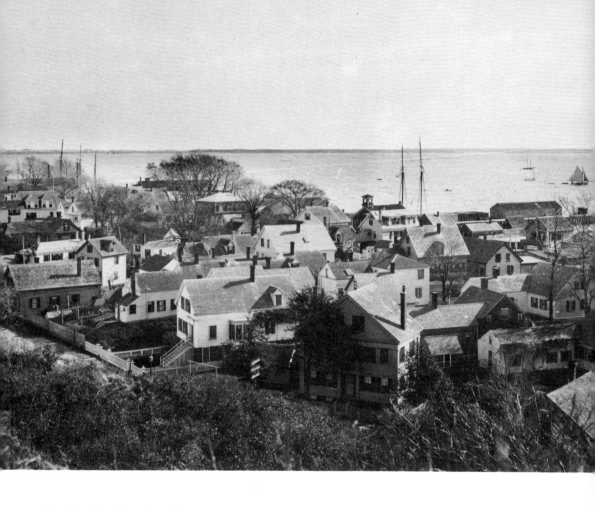

48. Overlooking Provincetown from High Pole Hill (10/22/03)

I love the sense in a small town of being able to hear all its activities from where you are sitting: the night crickets, the sound of gay voices in the back of town where a carnival is going on, and the barking of many dogs; and in the harbor a fishing boat thrumming its motor and a tug shrilling at a barge; on the railroad tracks, the evening train puffing back and forth, transposing its engine. T.W.

This was the very day one would have chosen to sit upon a hill overlooking sea and land, and muse there. The mackerel fleet was rapidly taking its departure, one schooner after another, and standing round the Cape, like fowls leaving their roosts in the morning to disperse themselves in distant fields. . . .

The Harbor of Provincetown—which, as well as the greater part of the Bay, and a wide expanse of ocean, we overlooked from our perch— is deservedly famous. It opens to the south, is free from rocks, and is never frozen over. It is said that the only ice seen in it drifts in sometimes from Barnstable or Plymouth. . . .

Probably Cape Cod was visited by Europeans long before the seventeenth century. It may be that Cabot himself beheld it. Verrazzani, in 1524, according to his own account, spent fifteen days on our coast, in latitude 41°40', (some suppose in the harbor of Newport,) and often went five or six leagues into the interior there, and he says that he sailed thence at once one hundred and fifty leagues northeasterly, *always in sight of the coast*. . . .

49. Looking east along the waterfront from a sandhill above the town (10/22/03)

I remember a night when the tides were so high that Wood End Point had been converted into a series of lagoons. The moon was up and the Bay was full of phosphorescence . . . As we followed the channels, which we could pick out because of their deeper color, we would sometimes scrape ever so gently against the sand, and hundreds of sand fleas, themselves alight with the phosphorous, would leap onto the beach, jumping quite a distance before their unaccustomed glory died. T.W.

By this time we saw the little steamer Naushon entering the harbor, and heard the sound of her whistle, and came down from the hills to meet her at the wharf. So we took leave of Cape Cod and its inhabitants. We liked the manners of the last, what little we saw of them, very much. They were particularly downright and good-humored. The old people appeared remarkably well preserved, as if by the saltness of the atmosphere, and after having once mistaken, we could never be certain whether we were talking to a coeval of our grandparents, or to one of our own age. They are said to be more purely the descendants of the Pilgrims than the inhabitants of any other part of the State. We were told that "sometimes, when the court comes together at Barnstable, they have not a single criminal to try, and the jail is shut up." It was "to let" when we were there. Until quite recently there was no regular lawyer below Orleans. Who then will complain of a few regular man-eating sharks along the back-side?

We often love to think now of the life of men on beaches,—at least in midsummer, when the weather is serene; their sunny lives on the sand, amid the beach-grass and the bayberries, their companion a cow, their wealth a jag of driftwood or a few beach-plums, and their music the surf and the peep of the beach-bird.

50. Along the waterfront from the beach at Provincetown (10/22/03)

We went to see the Ocean, and that is probably the best place of all our coast to go to. If you go by water, you may experience what it is to leave and to approach these shores; you may see the Stormy Petrel by the way, θαλασσοδρομα, running over the sea, and if the weather is but a little thick, may lose sight of the land in mid-passage. I do not know where there is another beach in the Atlantic States, attached to the mainland, so long, and at the same time so straight, and completely uninterrupted by creeks or coves or fresh-water rivers or marshes; for though there may be clear places on the map, they would probably be found by the foot traveler to be intersected by creeks and marshes; certainly there is none where there is a double way, such as I have de-scribed, a beach and a bank, which at the same time shows you the land and the sea, and part of the time two seas.

Footnotes for Introduction

1. Henry David Thoreau, *Cape Cod* (Cambridge: The Riverside Press, 1894), p. 1.
2. *The Journal of Henry David Thoreau* (Vols. VII-XX) of *The Writings of Henry David Thoreau*, ed. Bradford Torrey (Boston: Houghton Mifflin Company, The Riverside Press, Cambridge [1906], 20 volumes) 1850, p. 43.
3. *Ibid.*, September 7, 1851.
4. *Ibid.*, November 9, 1851.
5. *Ibid.*, May 10, 1853.
6. Herbert Wendell Gleason. *Through the Year with Thoreau: Sketches of Nature from the Writings of Henry David Thoreau with corresponding photographic illustrations* (Boston: Houghton Mifflin Co., The Riverside Press, 1917), p. 2.
7. *The Journal of H. D. Thoreau, opus cit.*, December 18, 1856.
8. *Ibid.*, February 27, 1857.
9. *Ibid.*, September 13, 1852.
10. *Ibid.*, May 13, 1857.
11. *Ibid.*, August 22, 1851.
12. *Ibid.*, September 2, 1851.
13. *Ibid.*, December 22, 1852.
14. *Ibid.*, November 2, 1858.
15. *Ibid.*, October 4, 1859.
16. *Ibid.*, November 10, 1860.
17. *Ibid.*, December 4, 1860.
18. *Ibid.*, December 12, 1859.
19. *Ibid.*, February 18, 1852.
20. *Ibid.*
21. *Ibid.*, February 19, 1852.
22. *Ibid.*, May 17, 1856.
23. *Ibid.*, May 18, 1856.
24. *Ibid.*, December 30, 1851.
25. *Ibid.*, February 18, 1857.
26. *Ibid.*, December 20, 1851.
27. *Ibid.*, May 22, 1854.
28. *Ibid.*, February 27, 1857.
29. *Ibid.*, December 3, 1859.
30. *Ibid.*, May 6, 1854.
31. Thoreau, *Cape Cod, opus cit.*, pp. 5–6.
32. *Ibid.*, pp. 7–9.
33. *Ibid.*, pp. 11–13.
34. *Ibid.*, pp. 2–3.
35. *Ibid.*, pp 245–246.

Index of Quotations used in captions and from Cape Cod